HOME WINEMAKING
Step - by - Step

A Guide to Fermenting Wine Grapes

Second Edition

Jon Iverson

Stonemark Publishing Co.

Home Winemaking Step-by-Step

Cover illustration: Susie Veon
Interior illustrations: Sarah Cribb
Book and cover design: Wellstone Press

ISBN 0-9657936-1-3

Second edition

Library of Congress Catalog Card No.
98-60601

Printed in the United States of America

STONEMARK PUBLISHING COMPANY
P.O. Box 687
Medford, OR 97501

CONTENTS

HOME WINEMAKING
Step-by-Step

QUANTITIES

Grapes - As a rule of thumb, 100 pounds of grapes will yield a gross total of 6 gallons (U.S.) of juice and pulp and a net of 5 gallons of finished wine after racking losses. This will vary depending on the relative water content of the grapes, how hard they are pressed, whether you settle out the pulp and ferment only the clear juice, and whether you use pectic enzyme, which will release more of the liquid but also create more pulp. Red grapes will usually yield slightly more because they are fermented on the skins and more liquid is released before pressing.

Sugar - If your must needs to be sweetened, $1^1/_2$ ounces of table sugar per U.S. gallon will raise the Brix by $1°$.

Acid - One level teaspoon per gallon of tartaric acid, malic acid or acid blend will raise the total acidity of a wine or must by approximately .12%. See *Appendix A* for testing total acidity and page 76 for further details on these acids.

Potassium metabisulfite - $^1/_4$ tsp. per 5 U.S. gallons = 50 parts per million (ppm). Use 50 ppm when crushing, 50 ppm at the first racking and 50 ppm when bottling.

INTRODUCTION

he first few chapters of this book will lead you successfully through the crushing, pressing, fermenting and clarifying steps of making white wines, as well as the bottling. White wines are a good place to start in understanding the art of fermenting wines, as it forces you to appreciate the pernicious effects of air. Minimize air contact, limit the use of meta, don't over–oak, and you will actually find it easier to make a good white wine than red.

There are a number of reasons white wines are easier than reds. The small amount of unfermented or "residual" sugar present in white wines tends to conceal flaws in the grapes and makes fruit quality less critical. In contrast, red wines are normally bottled "bone dry;" i.e., with no residual sugar. As a result, high acidity, low pH or flaws in the fruit quality are more easily detected in a finished red wine. The quality of the fruit has to be higher to make outstanding red wines.

White wines are also easier in that they are fermented cooler and are not as prone to spoilage problems during fermentation. Red grapes are normally fermented at higher temperatures in order to extract maximum flavor from the skins. The higher fermentation temperature increases the risk of spoilage and unwanted side reactions involving volatile acids.

In my experience, it has been easier to find quality white grapes than red, and at less cost. This will, of course, depend on the supply and demand situation in your area. The quality of white grapes seems to suffer less from the common practice of over–cropping than does the quality of red grapes. Since most white grapes ripen earlier than reds, the white grape crop is less often affected by early rains and frosts. If you have tried white wines in the past and had only marginal success, don't give up! Follow the basic procedures discussed in Chapter 1 through Chapter 5, and you'll be well rewarded.

If, as has been said, "the first duty of a wine is to be red," it follows that the first duty of a winemaker is to make red wines! The discussion of fermentation of red wines in Chapter 6, along with fermenting variations for red wines in Chapter 11 and malolactic fermentation in Chapter 12, covers all the techniques that can readily be used by a home winemaker.

You can make excellent red wines without going beyond Chapter 6, and I highly recommend that beginning winemakers do just that — stick to the basics in Chapter 6 and ignore the more advanced procedures discussed in Chapter 11 and Chapter 12. However, if you are a beginning winemaker intent on making red wines, be sure to read the earlier chapters on white winemaking. Some of the procedures are treated in greater detail there.

Glossaries of equipment and supplies are included at the end of several chapters. These are intended to be a reference source as needed. But not every term used in this book is fully defined. Just remember that "racking" means siphoning from one container to another and that potassium metabisulfite, meta, sulfite and SO_2 are synonyms, and you will get by very well!

Chapter One

GETTING STARTED

 he art of making wine has evolved a great deal in the last twenty or thirty years, and that applies to home winemaking as well as commercial. With the expanded array of equipment and supplies now available, the home winemaker can make routinely wines that exceed the quality of ordinary commercial wines. In fact, if you ferment the same grapes from the same vineyard, your wine should be better than the winery's! The home winemaker has an edge in working with small quantities and being able to clarify without having to pump and filter. The quality of your wine will be limited only by the quality of the grapes you crush and ferment.

Good grapes

This subject is as impossible as it is important! If omitted, the reader could legitimately ask why it was not included. So here goes. *The reason grape quality is so important is that good grapes are the basis for any good wine.* The better the grapes, the better the wine will be. Any honest vintner will admit that when the grapes come in good, the wine literally makes itself. It ferments without problems, clarifies readily and needs no adjustments before or after fermentation. On the other hand, if the grapes are poor, the best vintner in the world will not be able to make a great wine out of them.

There is no simple answer to the very elusive question of what makes a good grape. And it changes each year because growing conditions differ from year to year. Here are some general considerations, laden with my biases.

YIELD. Tons per acre is one of the biggest factors in determining quality. The growers like to believe that a heavy crop does not affect quality, as long as it ripens fully. Vintners believe that a light crop is inherently better than a heavy crop, and I side with the vintners. Historically, the best wines have come in years when Mother Nature imposed a low yield per acre. It is also significant that wineries growing their own grapes and making premium wines will intentionally drop fruit during the growing season.

VARIETY. Some varieties suffer more from over–cropping than others, chardonnay and pinot noir being two such that come to mind. Cabernet sauvignon and merlot are less affected and some of the other white varieties are even less affected. However, over–cropping always takes a toll. This means that if the yield looks to be 30% or 40% below normal, it should be a good year and you should start in early July trying to line up a source of grapes. It may take more effort because the wineries will compete harder for the reduced crop.

IRRIGATION. This is another subject on which the interest of the growers differs from the wineries. There is an inherent conflict of interest between the two in that the grower wants to maximize the yield and the winery wants the maximum quality. The problem is that few wineries are willing to pay the grower twice as much per pound for dropping half the grapes. So unless the grower has a contract with a winery, he will be inclined to water generously to increase the yield; but this dilutes quality. The plumper the grape, the higher the ratio of juice–to–skin. The best wines are thought to come from small berries because there is more skin surface relative to the volume of liquid. Although the best grapes probably come from grapes that have been dry–farmed, the effect of watering can be greatly reduced by stopping all irrigation during the six weeks prior to harvest. This allows the berries to shrink as harvest approaches.

SPECIFIC VINEYARDS. Due to a combination of factors, some vineyards will produce superior fruit year in and year out. The depth and composition of the soil are big factors. All else being equal, vines in shallow and poor soil are thought to produce better grapes than vines in deep, fertile soil. The availability of water is similarly related — grapes from a vineyard with abundant subterranean water will probably not measure up to those from a nearby vineyard with little underground water. Talk to vintners in your area to find out which vineyards and growers have the best reputation. I have found vintners to be as approachable and friendly as they are dedicated to their art!

Finding good grapes

The first order of business is lining up a source of good grapes. The earlier in the year you establish contact with possible sources, the more likely you will be rewarded with quality grapes in the fall. If you live in a grape growing region, start calling vineyards in early summer. By late June, they will know the extent of the fruit set and will be more willing to make a commitment. Some will want part of the money up front, which is a reasonable request if they are expected to reserve fruit for you. Some growers cater to home winemakers because they get top dollar for their fruit. And it's all cash to the grower, which isn't always the case when they sell to commercial wineries. So get on any mailing list that your inquiry uncovers.

Some wine supply stores make arrangements to buy grapes from growers and re–sell to amateurs. This convenience is worth the extra cost, and there is comfort in knowing that the grapes were likely picked at their peak. In the case of white grapes, some stores will even crush, press and sell you the juice, or "must" as it is called in winemaking parlance. This should have particular appeal to someone who plans to process small batches of grapes or who is uncertain about winemaking as a hobby. It saves the expense of purchasing or renting equipment.

The natural tendency is to want to ferment small quantities of several varieties. Although it is interesting to have several varieties, you will soon discover that it takes little more effort to process two or three hundred pounds of a given variety than one hundred pounds. A larger quantity also gives you the ability to ferment 5 gallons in one manner and 5 gallons in another. And starting with more, you are more likely to have a little left in two or three years, when the wine is reaching its peak! It is perfectly acceptable to ferment small batches; it's just that if you become serious about home winemaking, you will most likely lean toward larger quantities of fewer varieties.

Alternatives to fresh grapes

Most serious winemakers are probably reading the next section already. The rest of you, take note! There are some excellent juices available in forms which are not only easier to work with than fresh grapes but which generally eliminate the need for a crusher, crusher–stemmer or press. The reason I include this section is that many home winemakers do not live in wine growing regions. Even those who do will discover that locating a source of grapes is only the beginning. When the grapes ripen, there is a fairly short window of opportunity during which the grapes are at their peak and should be picked. This means that you might have to drop everything and go get them on short notice, often during the middle of the week. This very sizeable investment of time and planning can be circumvented by using frozen must, aseptic juice or concentrate kits rather than fresh grapes. If high quality grapes were used, some of these alternatives would probably make a better wine than fresh grapes of low quality. So, don't rule these alternatives out.

If fresh grapes were not available to me and I was intent on making high quality wine, my first choice would be frozen musts. These are grapes that have been crushed, sulfited and frozen. The buckets start thawing during shipment by UPS and can be fermented shortly after arrival. White grapes have been crushed *and* pressed. You ferment pure juice, so neither crusher nor press will be needed. Just follow the basic procedure for fermenting white wines as outlined in Chapter 2.

Red varieties arrive crushed and de–stemmed, so you will not need a crusher–stemmer. Just add a yeast starter and ferment in a primary fermenter for a few days, punching down as discussed in Chapter 6. A 5–gallon bucket of frozen must will yield about 3½ gallons of finished wine. A small press would be a convenience when the unfermented sugar has fallen to 0° Brix, but 5 gallons can easily be pressed in a nylon mesh bag. It requires a little more effort than a press, but you will get almost as much wine. And it is quicker to use rubber gloves and a nylon bag because there is no set up or clean up.

There should be no significant loss of quality as a result of freezing a must. Frozen musts are generally available on a first–come basis, so it tends to be a seasonal proposition. It will pay to get your name of the list early.

If frozen musts were not available, "aseptic" juices would be my next choice. If the same grapes were being processed, the quality should be only slightly lower than a frozen must. Rather than being frozen, the juice is flash pasteurized, sulfited, bagged and boxed. The juice has not been reduced in volume by boiling, as have the concentrates discussed below. Neither press nor crusher–stemmer is needed, even in the case of red grapes, as the skins have been processed and added back for pigment and complexity. After pasteurization, a controlled amount of sulfite is added and the juice is bagged and boxed. The home winemaker simply transfers the juice to a primary fermenter and ferments with no ado. No grapes to crush or de–stem, no punching down and no equipment to clean up! After being fermented in a primary fermenter for 3 or 4 days, the wine is transferred to carboys, topped with an air lock and allowed to ferment to dryness. Follow the basic procedure in Chapter 2. Bottle a red wine bone dry; sweeten a white wine slightly before bottling, as discussed in Chapters 3 and 4.

"Concentrate kits" are relatively new and superior in quality to the canned concentrates that have been around for decades. They are referenced as "kits" because they come packaged with all the essentials, such as sulfite, potassium sorbate, bentonite, isinglass or gelatin, oak flavoring, finishing agent and the like. Like aseptic juices, concentrate kits come bagged and boxed. However, after being flash pasteurized, they are reduced in volume by boiling at low temperatures in a vacuum. They are not reduced as much as the traditional canned concentrates; so the quality remains higher. Six gallons of juice might be reduced to 4 gallons or 3 gallons. The winemaker adds water back to bring the volume back up to 6 gallons and ferments according to directions. The shipping and storage costs are less, so the cost is less.

The traditional canned concentrates have been reduced the most in volume. The instructions typically call for adding 3 gallons of water to 1 gallon of concentrate. They have been processed longer than concentrate kits and probably subjected to more heat. Fruit quality being equal, the quality of canned concentrates should be lower.

Although some grapes of very high quality are sold as frozen musts, the very finest grapes will not be found in concentrates. Neither the processor nor the home winemaker could afford it. Grape quality is still critical, and some processors will use better grapes than others. In addition to grape quality, the sophistication of the industrial process used to make the concentrate is important to the ultimate quality. The better the vacuum, the lower the temperature at which the liquid will boil, and the less of the essence of the grape that is lost. Although all processors will trap the phenols and organic compounds that are boiled off and add them back before canning, a lower temperature and more gentle processing will retain more of these subtle organic compounds. Don't hesitate to ask questions about the processing before deciding on a concentrate.

See *Chapter 15* and *Appendix G* for more on fermenting aseptic juices and concentrate kits.

Equipment and supplies

You will also need to decide on equipment and supplies. Some items are essential at the outset, while certain others can wait until bottling or next year. Some are luxury items that you will never buy unless winemaking becomes a serious hobby.

The first stop should be your local winemaking supply store. If the Yellow Pages for your area have no listings under "beer and winemaking supplies," try a large metropolitan area. Call and ask for a catalog. Almost all wine supply shops have catalogs and are happy to ship. Shopping by mail is easy with toll–free numbers, FAX machines and UPS delivery.

If you will be fermenting aseptic juice or concentrates, you will not have to worry about the main pieces of winemaking equipment — the crusher and the press. If you plan to process only small quantities of fresh grapes to begin with, try renting a crusher and press, as the cash outlay to purchase is substantial. If you find yourself totally without access to equipment, small quantities of grapes can be crushed with a 4X4 post or even with your foot and pressed by hand in a nylon mesh bag! (Be careful, however, not to crack the seeds if crushing with a hard object, as they contain large amounts of highly–astringent tannin). But if you have much more than 100 pounds to process, try your best to borrow, rent or purchase a crusher and press.

Once you've made the decision to invest in equipment, try placing an ad in the "Miscellaneous Wanted" section of your newspaper classified ads. There are always retired home winemakers willing to part with used carboys, crushers and presses for much less than replacement cost. Most equipment lasts indefinitely, and used equipment is usually as functional as new. And whether you are considering new equipment or used equipment, the initial investment can be kept even lower and more fun had if several people go in together and pool their resources!

Equipment Glossary

The array of equipment available to the home winemaker has improved steadily over the years. It would take a tidy sum to buy everything at once, but you do not need everything at the outset in order to make quality wines. Here's a list of standard equipment and supplies. Note that plastic, polyethylene and polypropylene materials for pails, hoses and other materials that come in contact with the wine should be of food grade quality. This is indicated by a "USDA" or "HDPE" imprint. (Parentheses indicate that an item is not essential).

NOTEBOOK. Get a substantial notebook to keep notes. Some winemakers hang a tag around the neck of each carboy for immediately recording what was done and transfer the data to the permanent notebook later. Whatever technique you use, good notes are important.

CRUSHER. The threshold question in deciding on a crusher is whether you are primarily interested in white wines or red wines? For processing white grapes, a simple crusher with two meshed rollers is preferable to a crusher–stemmer.

CRUSHER

grape skins, stems, and juice

White grapes should be left on the stems for pressing, as the stems stabilize the mass inside the press and allow the juice to flow more freely.

A crusher–stemmer, however, is better for processing red grapes because the stems have to be separated before fermentation, and it does this automatically.

CRUSHER-STEMMER

stems

grape skins and juice

With a small quantity of red grapes, the stems can be fished out with a homemade rake, such as long stainless steel screws in a board, or even by hand. But with larger quantities, a crusher–stemmer is nearly indispensable. Unfortunately, crusher–stemmers are considerably more expensive than plain crushers, even if not motorized.

Whether you are looking at a plain crusher or a crusher–stemmer, consider getting a stainless steel hopper, as it is worth the extra cost in the long run. Washing and maintenance will be less critical, and you will not have to worry about contamination with trace amounts of metals.

PRESS. A good press is the other basic piece of winemaking equipment. The screw–type, vertical basket press of Italian origin has been around forever and works well. A basket of three to five gallon size is fine for 100 pound batches; but for larger quantities,

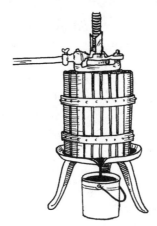

a larger basket will be appreciated. The No. 30 size — about 7.5 gallons — will press 150 pounds or more before it has to be split apart to dispose of the cake of skins and stems, which is called the "pomace." Bladder presses are better than the traditional press but considerably more expensive. And the bladders oxidize with age and have to be replaced, which is an extra expense.

Consider building or buying a stand to mount your press on. Not only will the press be more stable, but the added height will allow the use of larger containers to catch the juice as you press.

PRIMARY FERMENTERS. At least one primary fermenter will be needed. Red wines are initially fermented in an open container, preferably one with a lid or cover. Although white wines are best fermented in carboys, a primary fermenter will be needed anyway to hold the grapes and juice as they are crushed. And they are convenient for transporting grapes. So at least one primary fermenter, such as a Rubbermaid Brute®, should be on the shopping list.

A line of poly tanks manufactured by Graf and imported from Italy is available from some sources. They come in 60, 100 and 200 liter sizes and are ideal because they have a wide, screw–top lid with an air lock, plus a plug for draining. These tanks can be used as a primary fermenter for either white wines or red wines, with or without the skins. The wide mouth allows crushed grapes and juice to be poured in, making them an excellent choice for extended maceration or carbonic maceration of red grapes. Needless to say, the price is several times that of a plain "garbage can" of food quality.

If cost is not a factor, consider a 304 stainless steel vat with a floating lid. These containers are available in various sizes starting at 20 gallons. The lid has an inflatable tube around it, similar to a bicycle inner tube, which can be pumped up to make the fermenter airtight. Although a container of this type could be used to ferment almost any wine, it is especially desirable for carbonic maceration and extended maceration of red grapes after fermentation is complete.

PAILS. Two or three plastic pails will be needed to catch the juice as it flows out of the press, to dip crushed grapes, etc. Get the largest capacity pail that will slide under the drainage spout of the press. See *Illustration B*, page 26.

CARBOYS. The number needed will depend on how many grapes

you expect to be processing. One hundred pounds of grapes will yield roughly 6 gallons of unfermented must and pulp and 5 gallons of finished wine after loss of pulp and lees from several rackings. However, if you will be fermenting white wines and using carboys as primary fermenters, bear in mind that a 5–gallon carboy will accommodate only 60 to 70 pounds of grapes. That's because it can be filled only ¾ full, taking foaming into consideration. And an extra carboy will be needed for racking purposes.

Carboys come in 13, 7, 6, 5, 3 and 2.8 gallon sizes but some sizes are difficult to locate. After you have several 5–gallon carboys, get a 3–gallon carboy, or a 7 gallon carboy. You'll appreciate the flexibility year after year. You can never have too many carboys!

You will also need some smaller jugs to temporarily handle the excess volume — 1 gallon, 4 liter, 3 liter, 1.5 liter, etc. Make sure your stoppers will fit as the neck diameters of gallon jugs vary.

CARBOY STOPPERS. You will need one solid stopper per carboy and one drilled air lock stopper per carboy. Size no. 7 fits most carboys; no. 6½ fits most gallon jugs. Rubber stoppers are better than cork as they last indefinitely and don't lose their shape. Cork stoppers tend to assume the shape of the carboy neck and seat less dependably with age. Some stoppers made of newer synthetic materials, such as Dynaflex and Kraton, are elongated and will work in a wider range of neck diameters than rubber. Stoppers should be wrapped with a layer of sticky plastic wrap to counter the tendency to back out. Punch a hole in the plastic in the case of air locks.

AIR LOCKS. Several types of air locks or "bubblers" are available; all work acceptably well as long as the water level is maintained. The two–piece air lock with a straight stem and separate float requires less headspace above the carboy. It can also be used with a

½" vinyl hose to displace the air in a carboy before racking. *(Appendix C.)* It has the disadvantage of drawing reservoir liquid into the wine if the temperature falls, causing the volume to shrink. The one–piece, "S–shaped" air lock allows for backflow of air without contaminating the wine with reservoir liquid.

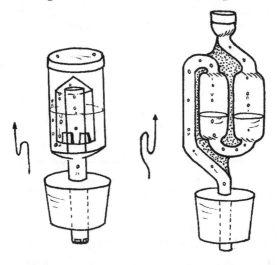

PLASTIC FUNNELS. Get the largest capacity you can find for racking into carboys. You will also need a smaller funnel to fit into wine bottles.

RACKING STEM, HOSE & CLIP. For racking from carboy to carboy, you will need a clear vinyl hose and racking stem of ⁵⁄₁₆", ³⁄₈" and/ or ½" diameter. If you get only one hose to begin with, the ³⁄₈" size would probably be best as it is good for siphoning and bottling. The ½" size is faster for racking and can also be used to funnel CO_2 from a fermenting carboy to an empty carboy to fill it with gas. *Appendix C.* Plastic clips are made which slip over the ⁵⁄₁₆" diameter to cut off the flow.

SACCHAROMETER, JAR AND WINE THIEF. This is basic equipment for testing the level of unfermented sugar in musts and sugar solutions. A wine thief is a convenience for lifting samples out of carboys.

BRUSHES. A carboy brush and a bottle brush are indispensable. Bend the carboy brush to fit the shoulder of the carboy.

WOOD DOWELS. Hardware store item. Used when stirring up lees to promote MLF, for topping in fining agents or meta rather than racking, etc. I have a very slender one for stirring up MLF lees and a heavy one for heavier jobs.

MEDICINAL TEASPOON. The ordinary kitchen teaspoon is amazingly inaccurate! They are often 30% more or less than a true teaspoon, which is approximately 5 ml. Greater accuracy is needed for measuring chemicals such as tartaric acid and meta. Get a medicinal teaspoon at the drug store, which can be used by trial and error to find a kitchen teaspoon that happens to be accurate. Then mark the kitchen version and use it to measure your chemicals by volume — it's much easier than weighing every time.

ACID TEST KIT. Total acid is such an important measurement in winemaking that you should invest in an acid test kit early in your home winemaking career. It will be well worth the modest cost. See *Appendix A* for details on assembling your own kit and conducting titration tests.

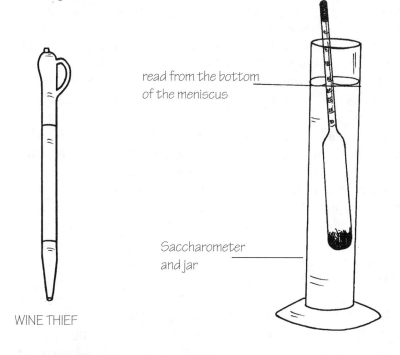

read from the bottom
of the meniscus

Saccharometer
and jar

WINE THIEF

CLINITEST TABLETS. These tablets for measuring residual sugar are available at some drug stores if your wine shop does not carry them. They are particularly important in making white wines in which small quantities of residual sugar are desired. See *Appendix A* for details on use.

PIPETS. Volumetric pipets are one of the most useful supply items. They can be used for Clinitest ($1/_2$ ml) and for acid titration tests (1 ml and 2 ml). When you are interested in controlling the addition of sulfite at bottling for instance, $1/_4$ tsp. of potassium metabisulfite can be dissolved in 25 ml of water and 1 ml dispensed into each bottle to give 50 ppm. They are exceedingly useful as a straw to sample wine right out of the carboy! Or out of the primary fermenter during extended maceration. A 5– or 10–ml size is needed to measure wine samples when doing titration tests with a burette. A 10–ml pipet also makes an ideal wine thief. A lab supply house will normally carry them if your wine supply shop does not.

(SCALE). Some type of scale capable of measuring fractions of an ounce (and preferably metric as well) is a convenience but by no means a necessity. A photographer's or reloader's scale would work, or even a digital postage scale. But you can get by without a scale. This book usually references chemicals in fractions of a teaspoon on the assumption that you will not have a scale.

(CO$_2$ TANK AND REGULATOR). Although it is possible to use a "CO$_2$ pot" to generate an inert gas (*Appendix C*), you are not likely to do it every time, due to the nuisance factor. If you plan to ferment a lot of white wines, a tank with a regulator is the answer to the air problem. White wines — and particularly those from hot climates — are so sensitive to air that every effort should be made to minimize the air contact. A tank makes it easy to displace the air. I have a small tank of argon with a regulator valve that reduces the flow to a few gallons per minute. Argon is heavier than nitrogen or carbon dioxide. The cost was less than $100 filled, at a welding supply shop.

(pH METER). Although it is not by any means a necessity, a pH meter will give you more insight into wine chemistry than any other piece of luxury equipment. You can quickly determine the effect on this all–important measurement of various procedures, such as increasing or decreasing the acid level, cold stabilization and malolactic fermentation, to name a few. The "digital revolution" has brought the price of pocket, digital pH meters down to approximately $100. They will read to $+/-$ .01 pH and are accurate to $+/-$ .02 pH, an impressive feat at the price.

Chemicals Glossary

POTASSIUM METABISULFITE. $^1/_4$ tsp./5 gal.= 50 parts per million (ppm); 1 t.= 6.3 g. Some people are allergic to sulfite and asthmatics are particularly sensitive to it. The fumes are highly caustic and care should always be taken to avoid breathing it or getting the solution in your mouth. Despite these disadvantages, I regard potassium metabisulfite, also referred to as "sulfite" or "meta," as the winemaker's best friend! Its virtues are many and impressive. It kills unwanted bacteria and foreign yeast but not cultured yeast. It inhibits enzymatic browning of white wines. It promotes clarification after fermentation is over. It stabilizes a white wine with residual sugar and discourages renewed fermentation. It extends the shelf life of your wine. And, at the right level, it actually improves the flavor. But don't use it indiscriminately. Low levels of meta will provide all the benefits.

Some winemakers like Campden tablets, which add about 75 ppm of sulfite at the rate of one tablet per gallon. But they have to be crushed with a mortar and pestle and even then are difficult to completely dissolve. The granular form of potassium metabisulfite is easier to use and less expensive.

TANNIN. Since white grapes have little or no tannin, a very small quantity ($^1/_4$ to $^1/_2$ tsp. per 5 gallons) should be added for astringency and as an aid in later fining with gelatin or isinglass.

PECTIC ENZYME. Pectic enzyme is commonly used in making fruit wines from apricots, peaches and other pit fruits. It can also be used for grape wines. It increases the yield of white grapes by breaking down the pulp and makes pressing and clarification easier. It aids in extracting flavors from the skins of red grapes by accelerating physical disintegration of the berry. Pectic enzyme loses it potency over time, so keep it refrigerated and replace it every 2 years. Follow manufacturer's recommended dosage. Note that enzymes will be rendered ineffective if bentonite is added at the same time.

POTASSIUM BITARTRATE. $^1/_4$ tsp./gal. Used as seed to hasten tartrate crystallization when cold stabilizing. Dissolve it in a quart of wine and stir it into the carboy with a dowel when the wine is at its coldest.

POTASSIUM SORBATE. Although it will not stop active fermentation, potassium sorbate will insure against renewed fermentation in wines bottled with higher levels of unfermented sugar. Add it at the rate of $3/4$ grams per gallon (200 ppm) and use it in conjunction with potassium metabisulfite for maximum effectiveness. It has a distinct flavor which some people dislike. Potassium sorbate is not needed for ordinary table wines having residual sugar of less than 1%. But if the grapes had *botrytis cinerea* and the wine was being bottled with 3% RS, for instance, it can be used as insurance against renewed fermentation. Potassium sorbate will generate a geranium–like odor disagreeable to most people if it is present during malolactic fermentation.

There are Glossaries after several succeeding chapters which should also be consulted:

Chapter Two

FERMENTING WHITE TABLE WINES

he basic process for making white table wines is as simple as it is universal. After the grapes are crushed and pressed, the juice is fermented in an enclosed container, free of air. Home winemakers typically ferment their white wines in partially–filled carboys topped with an air lock. After most of the sugar has been fermented and the frothy stage of fermentation is past, the carboys are topped up and allowed to ferment to complete dryness. After it is dry, the wine is clarified, the residual sugar and total acid are corrected, and it is bottled. The commercial winery will filter at least once in addition to gravity fining, and it may age the wine in oak casks for a period of time. But the basic procedure is otherwise the same for both.

Sterilizing solution

The first step in the new fermenting season should be the preparation of a jug of sulfite solution. It is easier to always have a jug of sterilizing solution ready when racking or cleaning equipment than having to mix a new solution every time. It will be used repeatedly throughout the season. The exact concentration is not critical, so start with 1 tablespoon of potassium metabisulfite dissolved in a gallon of water. The solution can be re–used; after rinsing out a carboy, for instance, just funnel it back into the jug. When it gets low, top it up with more water and meta. If it picks up too much sediment, mix a new solution.

Culling out bad fruit

Before being crushed, the grapes should be examined carefully and any rotten clusters discarded. If a cluster is raisined and hard, discard it and proceed using only fruit that is of sound quality. Sometimes there will not be a bad cluster in the whole lot; at other times, culling out the bad fruit can be tedious. But it is important with white wines. Resist the temptation to wash the fruit as it probably would not remove any residual sprays and would only set the stage for unwanted mold and infection.

Preparing a yeast starter solution

A yeast starter solution should be initiated as soon as the grapes or juice arrive. Spontaneous or "natural" fermentation — the process of crushing and pressing without sulfite and letting natural yeast on the grapes and in the air establish and do the fermenting — is fashionable with some commercial vintners. But it's not recommended for the home winemaker, particularly with white wines. It takes too long for natural yeast to multiply to the point where they start converting the sugar to alcohol, and the result is too uncertain. In addition, most strains of wild yeast will not ferment to complete dryness because they are killed off by low alcohol levels. Use one of the many strains of cultured wine yeast and you will get better results.

There are two steps involved in building a yeast starter solution, the first being to activate the packet of dry yeast. Start with 1/2 cup of warm water — about 90°. Sprinkle the yeast granules over the surface, without stirring. It will be re–hydrated in minutes.

The second step is increasing the volume. This is best done by squeezing or mashing up a cup of fresh grape juice and diluting it with a cup of water to lower the sugar level. (Diluted because yeast multiply faster with medium sugar concentration than high). Add a pinch of diammonium phosphate ("D.A.P.") to stimulate multiplication. Mix the yeast cup and diluted grape juice together in a carafe or jar, plug it with cheesecloth and set it atop the hot water heater or in a warm window sill. This should all be accomplished within 15 – 30 minutes after the yeast was hydrated. The starter solution will be actively fermenting in an hour or two.

The $1\frac{1}{2}$ pints of yeast starter solution thus concocted will be sufficient to inoculate 10 gallons of must at the optimum starter–to–must ratio of 2%. A larger volume of starter could be used, but that would needlessly dilute the wine. If you have more than 10 gallons of must to ferment and need more than $1\frac{1}{2}$ pint of starter, start with 2 or 3 cups of fresh juice, dilute with an equal volume of water, and follow the same procedure. Always wait until the starter is fermenting actively before inoculating.

Normally, one prefers to work with dry yeasts as they are easier. However, some excellent yeast strains exist which are available only in liquid form. The procedure for activating a liquid yeast is basically the same, but it might take longer to become active to the point where it can be used to inoculate the must. With a slow–fermenting liquid yeast sample, such as Steinberg, start two or three days before the grapes are to arrive. You want the starter to be active and ready to go when the grapes are crushed and pressed so as to minimize the delay before fermentation.

Start with $\frac{1}{2}$ cup of freshly–pressed juice from oranges, grapefruits or Thompson seedless grapes and dilute with $\frac{1}{2}$ cup of water. Don't use canned or pasteurized juices as they might contain preservatives which would inhibit yeast growth. Bring the diluted juice to a brief boil to kill the wild yeast. After it has cooled, add a pinch of D.A.P. and the liquid yeast sample. Cover the carafe or jar with cheesecloth and set it in a warm place. It might take a couple of days, but it will eventually become active. It helps after about 24 hours to pour it back and forth into another container for aeration. Yeast like air during the multiplication stage. (But when they reach maximum concentration and start converting the sugar to alcohol, air should be eliminated).

When the grapes arrive, add a cup of the freshly–pressed grape juice plus a cup of water to increase the volume. Put it back in the warm spot until it is active again and ready to add to the must a few hours later.

Of course, if you already have wine fermenting and want to use the same strain of yeast for the next batch of grapes, it's even easier to get a starter. Just siphon a cup or two of the lees off the bottom of the fermenting must and add it to some fresh grape juice diluted with water. It will be active shortly.

Cleanliness

Cleanliness is important but not in the sense that a beginning winemaker might expect. Don't worry about a few earwigs and spiders! They'll end up in the lees just like the dead yeast cells. Nor is a little dirt any cause for concern. My point is not to encourage a disregard of cleanliness but to emphasize the principal concern of a home winemaker — AIR. Without air as the catalyst, most dirt, bacteria and other potential sources of spoilage remain innocuous. If you want to be a fanatic about something, let it be air rather than dirt. Minimize air contact at all times and you are not likely to experience spoilage problems.

Yes, the equipment should be clean, but it need not be surgically sterile. If the crusher and press were cleaned after the last use and show no signs of mold, it will suffice to hose them down. If they look dirty, they should be scrubbed and then sprayed with some of your sulfite solution in a hand sprayer. Some winemakers religiously sulfite everything that comes in contact with their wine. But if my equipment is clean, I normally just hose it down and have not had problems with spoilage. That's probably because I am a fanatic about air.

Crushing

The grapes should be crushed as soon as possible after being picked and fermentation initiated with as little delay as possible. White grapes should be crushed on the stems as the stems stabilize the mass in the press and facilitate drainage of the juice. A simple crusher with two rollers, mounted over a primary fermenter or other receptacle, is all that one needs for crushing white grapes. *Illustration A.* If you have a crusher–stemmer, remove the de–stemming trough. If you cannot disable the de–stemmer, mix some stems back in before pressing.

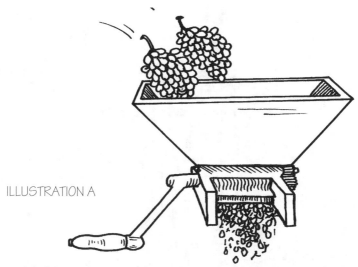

ILLUSTRATION A

After crushing, the grapes go into a large pail or primary fermenter of food grade quality. A small amount of potassium metabisulfite, or "meta" as I usually refer to it, is carefully measured, dissolved in an ounce or two of water and thoroughly mixed in. The dosage will depend on the condition of the grapes.

For grapes in good condition having normal sugar, acid and pH, the recommended dosage of meta is 1/4 tsp. per 5 gallons of volume, which is roughly 50 parts per million (ppm). If your grapes are high in sugar, low in acid and presumably have a high pH, the dosage should be increased to 1/2 tsp. Use of more than 120 ppm is not advisable unless the grapes are badly sunburned, have broken skins, bunchrot or are in extremely poor condition, which hopefully will not be the case.

Contrary to its current image, meta is a great preservative and anti–oxidant and will help keep the must from browning. It kills natural yeast and bacteria but has little effect on cultured yeast at levels under 50 ppm. Don't hesitate to use it. On the other hand, never use more than necessary. Keep accurate records as to how much meta was added to each batch of wine and when. Be aware that an unfermented must will accommodate more meta than a finished wine. And a wine will handle larger doses of meta right after fermentation, when it still contains solids, than it will after clarification. In my experience judging at county fairs, excess meta

ILLUSTRATION B

is the most common mistake of home winemakers. They add too much, too late in the game.

Some winemakers also add pectic enzyme at the time the grapes are crushed. I use it for red wines to accelerate breakdown of the berry and extraction of flavor. I normally do not use it for white wines except when I soak the crushed grapes on the skins — it breaks down the pulp, makes pressing easier and increases the yield. See page 81.

Pressing

Dip the crushed grapes and juice out of the primary fermenter with a small pail and pour them into the press basket. It is not necessary to line the basket with cheesecloth or fiberglass mesh in pressing *vinifera* grapes but one certainly could, as is commonly done in pressing the very slippery *labrusca* grapes. Compact the mass as much as possible by hand, then add more grapes, compress by hand again. When the basket is nearly full, put the wood blocks and screw in position and start applying mechanical pressure. When you meet stiff resistance and the flow diminishes to a trickle, take a break. Have another sip of last year's effort! The flow will stop completely in a few minutes and then you can start cranking again. Repeat the cycle of pressing and waiting until it has been pressed to your satisfaction.

When it has been fully pressed, reverse the pawls (*Illustration B inset*), back off the screw and remove the blocks. Then discard the pomace. Reassemble the basket and repeat the process.

The grapes can actually be pressed two or three times to maximize the yield — fluff them up and start over. Additional pressings are certainly worthwhile if you pressed whole clusters without crushing first in order to minimize skin contact. The grapes in the center of the mass will still contain some juice. However, if you crushed, used pectic enzyme and soaked on the skins before pressing, additional pressings will not increase the yield very much; you will get almost all of the fermentable juice with one hard pressing.

Adding yeast starter

Since the goal is to get fermentation under way as quickly as possible, the must should be inoculated as soon as the yeast starter is active. The only caveat is that inoculation should be delayed for 30 minutes after sulfiting to give the sulfite time to bond with the solids and impurities in the must. Cultured yeasts are somewhat sensitive to sulfite, but after a few minutes will not be affected. However, if you had to give your grapes an unusually heavy dose of meta because they were in poor condition, wait several hours before inoculating.

If your starter is not visibly active by the time you are through crushing, store the must in a cool place while waiting for the starter to become so. It's a good idea to keep a couple of gallon ice jugs ready in the freezer in case you run into an extended delay in getting your starter active — just tighten the caps, drop the jugs in and stir the must occasionally to cool it throughout.

To inoculate, just sprinkle the starter solution over the surface of the must. This allows air contact, which stimulates yeast multiplication. Don't stir it, as that would disperse the concentration of yeast, reduce exposure to air and slow down multiplication. After you see signs of fermentation, it can be stirred if you wish; but even then, stirring is not necessary.

Since white grapes are low in nutrients, some winemakers add a balanced yeast food, D.A.P., yeast hulls, yeast extract, or the like when pressing. I do this with chardonnay grapes, which are said to be the most nutrient–deficient of the white varieties. I also add yeast food if I suspect that the grapes contain residual sulfur. The nitrogen in the yeast food reduces the tendency to generate H_2S toward the end of fermentation. But yeast food is generally not necessary for *vinifera* grapes. If fermentation is reluctant to start, it is almost always the result of too much sulfite, inoculating before the starter is fully active or low temperature rather than lack of nutrients.

Temperature is a major consideration when attempting to initiate fermentation. Since yeast multiply faster under warm conditions, the temperature should be maintained at 65 – 70° until fermentation starts. The temperature can be lowered after fermentation is underway if you want to cool ferment. I usually initiate fermentation of white wines at room temperature and then move the carboys outdoors once it starts.

Testing total acid and sugar

The sugar and acidity of the must should be tested as soon after pressing as possible. Always take and record these two readings — after pressing but before fermentation starts. *Appendix A.* A saccharometer is the only item needed to check the sugar level. The sugar content of white wine grapes should be in the range of 18° – 24° Brix, depending on the variety.

A titration test kit for testing total acid is inexpensive and easy to use. The total titratable acid would ideally be between 6 to 9 grams/liter before fermentation, and closer to 6 than 9. I usually refer to acid readings as percentages, such as .6% or .9%. *See Appendix A for details on conducting titration tests.*

Adjusting acid level

Hopefully, the acid level of the must will be in the desired range and adjustments will not be needed. But sometimes, due to weather or timing of the pick, the acid level will be off. In hot climates, the sugar level can shoot past the desired level in one or two days, resulting in low acid. In any climate, rain or unseasonably cold weather can hamper ripening so that sugar and acid never do reach the desired levels. Humidity can cause mold and force pre–mature harvesting. There are several ways to raise acidity (Chapter 8) and several ways to lower it (Chapter 9).

If the acid level of the must is much outside the desired range of .6% to .9%, it will probably need to be adjusted. The question is whether to make the adjustment before fermentation or after fermentation and cold stabilization? One would normally prefer to adjust before fermentation because that gives the additives a chance to blend with the natural constituents during fermentation and for the byproducts to precipitate. A larger correction can be made before fermentation without affecting flavor.

On the other hand, the acid level falls naturally during fermentation and cold stabilization but by an unpredictable amount — usually in the range of .05 to .10%, but sometimes more. The final acid level is even more uncertain if you plan to put the wine through malolactic fermentation. You run the risk of over–correcting by adjusting before fermentation. To avoid this possibility, I normally make a partial correction before fermentation, if the readings are well off the mark; i.e., raise it to .6% or lower it to 1.0% or .9% before fermentation if it is outside the range. A smaller correction can be made after fermentation and cold stabilization if necessary. On the other hand, if the must acidity is between .6% and .9%, it is better to wait until after fermentation and cold stabilization to make a correction.

Adjusting sugar

The practice of adding sugar, known as chaptalization, is common in Germany and other regions where grapes have difficulty ripening and sometimes have to be picked with sugar as low as 17° Brix. Whether or not sugar should be added depends on the level of natural sugar in the must, the grape type and the style of wine to be made. If you are crushing chardonnay or sauvignon blanc grapes with low sugar and want a dry table wine, the sugar should be raised to 20 or 21° Brix. Just stir it in — 1½ ounces of ordinary table sugar per gallon will raise the Brix by 1°. This can be done at your leisure while waiting for fermentation to commence, or even shortly after fermentation starts.

The sugar level is less critical in the case of other white grapes, such as reisling, gewurtztraminer and semillon, particularly if your goal is a semi–sweet wine. But even then, I would raise the sugar level by 1° or 2° if it is below 18° Brix after crushing and pressing.

Fermenting in carboys

At some point, the must will be poured into carboys. Some winemakers let it ferment two or three days in an open primary fermenter before transferring to carboys. My preference is to transfer as soon as fermentation starts. The carboys should be filled only three–fourths full. The air space is needed to allow room for foaming. A certain amount of foaming always accompanies fermentation, but it can be quite dramatic with certain vigorous yeasts under warm conditions and in musts containing large amounts of pulp. Note that fermentation could also be initiated in the carboy (¾ full), but it will take longer to start because the must has less exposure to air. You might have to aerate it if fermentation is reluctant to start.

Fermentation should start in 24 to 36 hours; if not, see *Appendix B*. Once fermentation starts, the must should be deprived of oxygen. In fact, avoidance of air contact should become your guiding

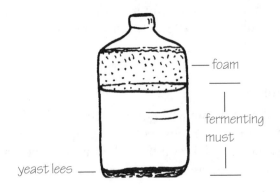

foam

fermenting must

yeast lees

principle from now until the wine is finally bottled and corked in six or eight months. Substitute an air lock for the cheesecloth. Pour sulfite solution in the reservoir of the air lock to help discourage the fruit flies.

Controlling fermentation

After fermentation starts, the goal changes. Whereas the initial goal was to get fermentation initiated as quickly as possible, now the goal is to avoid "runaway" fermentation. If a vigorous yeast is used under warm fermenting conditions, it could ferment to complete dryness in 3 or 4 days. That's too fast — too much of the bouquet and complexity is lost. Overly vigorous fermentation can be avoided by using a slower yeast or by lowering the temperature of the must.

The ideal temperature range for fermenting most white wines is 50–60°. In this range, it will take ten days or more for the sugar to ferment down to 10° B. At this slower rate, the loss of bouquet is minimized and more of the fruit flavor is retained. When deciding where to ferment, look for the coolest place you can find. If you do not have an air conditioned corner of the house, the basement would be fine. Garages are often used but they can get hot in the fall. I frequently ferment white wines outside on the north side of the house. However, if temperatures in the 80s or 90s are encountered, a way should be found to cool the must.

Fermentation will start rather slowly but will quickly gather momentum. The most vigorous fermentation will occur when the sugar is dropping from 20° Brix to 10° Brix. Fermentation should be monitored daily during this stage. Lift a sample out of the carboy with a wine thief. If the sugar level appears to be falling by more than 5° per day as fermentation speeds up, find a way to cool it. You could make a cold water bath by setting the carboys in a tub or wading pool with running tap water. If your tap water is too warm, drop in a block of ice or milk jugs with frozen water once or twice a day. It is only the extreme afternoon heat that is cause for concern as the night air will cool.

Once the sugar level drops below 10° B., you can relax. The frothy, tumultuous stage is over. With the higher alcohol content and lowered sugar level, fermentation will slow no matter what the temperature or what the yeast type.

Always be alert to possible "rotten egg" smell during or after fermentation, which indicates hydrogen sulfide. Immediate corrective action should be taken if it is encountered. *Appendix B.* Note, however, that some yeasts, most notably Montrachet, will generate a mild hydrogen sulfide odor. This is usually not a problem as it will disappear after one or two rackings. It is a pronounced and unmistakable rotten egg odor that is cause for concern.

Combining carboys

When the saccharometer indicates that unfermented sugar is approaching 0° Brix, the carboys should be combined and filled to the top. There will still be around 2% unfermented sugar when the saccharometer reads 0° Brix. You want the carboys to be full when the wine falls still and CO_2 is no longer being produced to dispel air. If the unsightly muck on the neck and shoulders of the carboy doesn't bother you, just top up — the muck might look gross but will not affect wine quality. It would be equally acceptable to rack into clean carboys.

Unless H_2S was encountered, you can use the "mud" and pulp on the bottom if more liquid is needed to fill the last carboy. It's also acceptable to top up with a similar wine of good quality. There will seldom be any defects in a wine at this early stage, but note that it is always good practice to taste each carboy before two different lots are blended or combined. If one happened to have flaws, both batches would probably be ruined by blending.

Juggle the volumes as needed to fill a lesser number of carboys. As a result of combining carboys, three fermenting carboys will become two; or four will become three, as the case may be. This is where it becomes convenient to have carboys in a variety of sizes, such as 2.8, 3, 5 and 7 gallon sizes. A few jugs and larger bottles — 1 gallon, 3 liter, 4 liter, 1.5 liter — should also have been located ahead of time to accommodate the excess volume. Top the jugs with an air lock and allow them to ferment to dryness along with the carboys. Small, drilled air lock stoppers are made which will even allow you to ferment in wine bottles. Every container should be as full as possible so as to minimize air contact. The smallest container can be topped with water if necessary. The point is to take no chances with air.

This is also a good time to add a little tannin, which white grapes lack. If you plan to add oak chips of some type, the tannin in the oak will be sufficient. If not, $1/4$ to $1/2$ tsp. of tannin per 5 gallons could be added, first dissolved in an ounce or two of water. This small amount will add a bit of astringency to the wine and will be helpful in later clarification efforts involving isinglass or gelatin. If malolactic fermentation is on your agenda, you can add the starter now, being sure to maintain a temperature of 65° or more until the process is complete. See Chapter 12 — *Malolactic Fermentation.*

After the carboys have been combined, the wine should be allowed to ferment to dryness. Since this might take several weeks at temperatures below 60°, I normally finish fermentation at room temperature. This not only assures uninterrupted and complete fermentation but saves several weeks of fermenting time and allows for earlier bottling. A warmer temperature is also needed to support malolactic fermentation if that is desired. If you have been cold fermenting outside, this would mean lugging the carboys inside.

Raising the temperature is not mandatory as the wine will usually ferment to dryness but over a longer period. But note that a nearly finished wine should not be subjected to temperatures below 50° for an extended period of time. It might get "stuck" with a few points of unfermented sugar, and it could be difficult to re–initiate fermentation in the spring.

The wine will normally be dry when the bubbles stop, but this should be confirmed with Clinitest. *Appendix A.* Clinitest tablets are the only practical way to check residual sugar; a saccharometer will not accurately measure unfermented sugar because the alcohol level has altered the density of the liquid. You cannot rely on your palate right after fermentation as the wine is still too yeasty. Clinitest is the answer. As long as the residual sugar is below .1% or .2% (dark blue–green on the Clinitest chart), consider it dry, even though trace amounts of various unfermented sugars will always remain.

Cold stabilization

After fermentation is complete, the carboys should be topped up again if necessary and moved to a cool or cold place while the dead yeast cells, pectins and various byproducts of fermentation, called the "gross lees," settle out. The wine will be racked and fined several times during the next six months to promote clarification. But first, the gross lees should be allowed to settle out, preferably at a cool or cold temperature. A walk–in cooler would be great for cold stabilizing but is by no means necessary. It works as well to leave the carboys outside or in the garage.

After all effervescence has stopped, replace the air lock with a solid rubber stopper wrapped with a layer of sticky plastic wrap. Cap it with a fruit jar to keep the rain out if it is being left outdoors. The wine will not freeze as long as its temperature stays above 25° F.

There is little to do during cold stabilization other than watching to see if the rubber stopper is forced out. An increase in temperature could force the stopper out, so once is not necessarily cause for concern. But if it keeps popping out, this is a signal that microbes are busy at work, converting H_2S into mercaptans and disulfides. The minute volume of gas produced in the process cannot be detected with an air lock, but it will force the stopper out. That's why it is a good idea to substitute a stopper for the air lock at the earliest opportunity. A popped stopper is the best indicator I have found of unwanted activity in the carboy. See *Appendix B.*

After cold stabilizing for one to two months, the gross lees and tartrate crystals will have settled and clarification will have come to a near standstill. The wine is ready for the first racking.

Yeasts Glossary

Many different strains of yeast are readily available to the home winemaker. Lallemand, Gist–brocades and Red Star collectively dominate the market. Vierka also markets an extensive line of dry and liquid yeasts but many cannot be identified beyond the marketing name, such as "Sauternes." Although I have found the yeasts to be dependable, the nomenclature could be misleading to someone inclined to assume that the yeast type will determine the wine type. Nothing could be further from the truth. Wyeast Labs of Mt Hood, Oregon has a new line of liquid yeasts in foil pouch ("Vintners Choice") that are easy to activate. The line includes Steinberg and other yeasts that in dry form can be difficult to activate.

Much has been written about the different flavor characteristics the various strains of yeasts impart. Differences undoubtedly exist immediately after fermentation, and they matter greatly to the commercial winery, which does not want to tie up its fermentation capacity too long and wants its wines to be marketable as soon as possible. But the differences are minor from the home winemaker's viewpoint. Two years after a wine has been bottled, I doubt whether anyone would be able to tell the difference anyway.

Selection of yeast strain is nevertheless interesting and sometimes can be important. If, for instance, the Brix of the must is abnormally high, and you want a dry wine, pick a strain that is tolerant of high alcohol, such as Prise de Mousse or Pasteur Champagne. Do not use Epernay 2 as it is not very tolerant of high alcohol. If the grapes have *botrytis cinerea*, higher levels of sulfite should be used. Since the Brix will probably be higher, use one which is tolerant of high sulfite and high alcohol, like Prise de Mousse. If you want to cold ferment a white wine, use a cold–tolerant yeast, such as Epernay 2, Prise de Mousse or, my preference, Steinberg. If you want to stop fermentation with some residual sugar, use a less vigorous strain, which would again be Steinberg or Epernay 2, and deprive it of nutrients as well. If you suspect that the grapes have residual sulfur on them, do not use Montrachet as it is particularly prone to converting the sulfur into hydrogen sulfide.

Here is a brief description of the more common strains, including marketing names and the U.C. Davis number where applicable.

PRISE DE MOUSSE (Red Star, Premier Cuvée; Lalvin, EC1118). This
vigorous dry yeast is good for either reds or whites, including
cooler fermenting temperatures. It has become very popular with
commercial wineries due to its willingness to ferment to completion with few problems. It has little effect on the varietal characteristic of the grape, which can be either a positive or negative,
depending on the result desired. Prise de Mousse is a good yeast
to re–initiate a stuck fermentation and for *tirage* fermentation of
sparkling wines because it is tolerant of alcohol. It is a very low
foamer and does not have the tendency of Montrachet to generate
hydrogen sulfide. However, it might be more difficult to initiate
malolactic fermentation if this yeast is used.

MONTRACHET (UCD #522) is quite vigorous and produces a finished wine, red or white, with excellent complexity. It remains one
of my favorites for red wines, chardonnay and even
gewurtztraminer. However, it is prone to produce hydrogen sulfide, particularly if the grapes had residual sulfur on them.

PASTEUR RED This is an excellent general purpose yeast for full–
bodied red wines, such as cabernet sauvignon and red Rhone varieties. It produces full–bodied, complex wines and has been a standard of commercial wineries for many years.

PASTEUR CHAMPAGNE (UCD #595). This is an all–purpose yeast
commonly used for white wines. It is not used to make sparkling
wines, however. It has good vigor, leaves a pleasant yeasty flavor,
and generates moderate foam.

CALIFORNIA CHAMPAGNE (UCD #505). I wish Red Star still marketed this fine yeast for white wines in 5–gram packets. It is ideal
for the *tirage* fermentation of champagnes because it coagulates
and clarifies very readily. In fact, it is a good all–round yeast for
white wines in general. It is available seasonally in prepared form
from some sources.

EPERNAY 2 (Red Star, Côtes de Blanc). This medium–speed yeast
emphasizes the fruit in either reds or whites. Epernay is sometimes
used to ferment reislings or gewurtztraminers intended to have some

residual sugar as it tends not to ferment all the way to dryness at cool temperatures; i.e., it tends to get stuck late in fermentation. It is not very tolerant of high alcohol levels. It often leaves a "soapy" taste shortly after fermentation but it eventually dissipates.

STEINBERG (Geisenheim Inst.) ferments slowly and is ideal for cold fermenting a white wine over a long period of time. It produces a wine with good complexity and structure. It is my favorite for cool fermentation of white wines. It slows but does not completely stop at temperatures below 50°. It can be difficult to activate Vierka's liquid sample. Lallemand markets it in dry form as part of its Uvaferm line, but I have not seen it in 5-gram packets.

Many other strains of yeast are available, including a growing list of Lalvin yeasts by Lallemand. Some must be ordered in prepared form from a wine supply distributor during season. Others are available in 5–gram packets.

Note that "dry" does not mean freeze–dried; so don't put your yeasts in the freezer as you would freeze–dried malolactic packets. Dry yeasts store best at cool temperatures, such as the wine cellar.

Yeast Supplements Glossary

DIAMMONIUM PHOSPHATE (D.A.P.) 1/2 – 3/4 g. per gallon. 1 tsp. = 4.3 g. The legal limit of this nitrogen source is 3.6 g. per gallon but much less will suffice. It is very effective in stimulating yeast growth but usually is not necessary. It is good for making yeast starter solutions and in musts that are nutrient deficient, such as chardonnay or musts that have been pre–fined and settled before fermentation. A dose of D.A.P. when inoculating adds a bit of insurance against hydrogen sulfide if the grapes had residual sulfur on the skins.

YEAST EXTRACT 1/2 g. per gallon. This is a very good source of nitrogen for budding yeast cells. Malolactic bacteria like yeast extract as well.

YEAST HULLS, or "ghosts." 1.3 g. per gallon. This is the cell membranes of yeast — the innards became yeast extract. The hulls affect some of the acids in a way that promotes fermentation.

BALANCED YEAST FOOD. Various blends of the above are marketed. They usually contain yeast vitamins as well, such as B–1, thiamin and vitamin H. I only use this more expensive supplement on the rare occasions when I need to re–inoculate a stuck fermentation.

Chapter Three

RESIDUAL SUGAR AND TOTAL ACID

 efore continuing with procedure, a little theory is in order. If there is any one secret to making good white wines, it would have to be the amount of unfermented or residual sugar (RS) in the finished wine relative to total acid (TA). Wines will often ferment to .05% residual sugar, but white wines should not be bottled that dry. A bone–dry white wine might seem well balanced at a very young age. This is because the fruitiness in a new wine has the same effect on the palate as sugar — it counters the acidity. But as the fruitiness diminishes over time, a bone–dry white wine will become increasingly astringent and unappealing. A bit of sugar is needed to keep it softer and fruitier and will be particularly appreciated after the wine has aged a while. The sugar also enhances the bouquet and brings out more of the varietal characteristic of the grape.

There are two ways to control the amount of residual sugar in the finished wine. One way is to ferment it to complete dryness, and then add back a measured amount of sugar or reserve must, as contemplated in Chapters 2 and 4. The other way is to stop fermentation before all the sugar has fermented, as discussed in Chapter 10.

The correct amount of residual sugar is largely a matter of personal preference, and the amount will also vary with the level of acid, the mix of acids, the grape type, the pH and the style of wine sought. Titration readings, while helpful, do not tell the whole story. Some wines with acidity of .65%, for example, will taste tarter than others having the same acidity (and the same residual sugar). This is because the ratio of various acids differs from wine to wine, and some acids taste more sour than others. In addition, a varying portion of the total acidity in a finished wine will be attributable to tartrate salts, which are less sour than tartaric acid itself. These variables make the residual sugar decision as much a matter of art as science, even for a commercial vintner. Rely on your taste buds as much as the titration readings when deciding on the level of residual sugar for a particular wine. And remember that the wine will taste tarter as the fruitiness diminishes with age.

Here are some very general parameters for your initial guidance in balancing residual sugar and total acid. With a finished white table wine having total acidity in the normal .65–.70% range, few people could distinguish between .1% RS and .4% RS; both would taste "dry" to almost all. Unless you have a strong bias in favor of very dry white table wines, the minimum level of residual sugar should probably be around .2 or .3%, assuming normal acid. But again, it will depend on the grape type. Chardonnay and sauvignon blanc, for instance, are often made drier than other varieties. If you like your wines with some noticeable sweetness, you would want residual sugar of .75 –1%, or even more.

One "rule of thumb" for table wines is to match the residual sugar with the total acid. If the acidity in the still wine is .65%, raise the residual sugar to .65%, at which point a touch of sweetness would be noticeable, again depending on the mix of acids. Matching the residual sugar and total acidity happens to be the rough dividing line below which residual sugar is not very discernible to most people and above which it quickly becomes noticeable. This rule of thumb works only when acidity is in the normal range. If acidity is high, say 1.0%, residual sugar might have to be raised well above 1% to reach the sweetness threshold. On the other hand, if the acid is on the low side, let's say, .55 to .60%, residual sugar of .2% might result in a well–balanced, dry table wine. After going through malolactic fermentation, chardonnays are typically bottled with total acid of approximately .6% and residual sugar in the range of .2% or less.

Given the absence of any hard and fast rules for balancing residual sugar and total acidity, I highly recommend routinely testing them in the various commercial wines that you like, as well as your own. And keeping notes. This will help you define your palate and facilitate a better guess as to how much residual sugar you want in a particular wine relative to the acid.

Chapter Four

First Racking

fter several weeks of cold stabilizing, the wine will cease to clarify further. This will normally take four to six weeks but could take up to two months. The wine will be much clearer but will still be visibly hazy. Crystals of precipitated potassium bitartrate might be visible in the lees. The exact timing of the first racking is not critical, but the longer it is left on the fermentation lees, the greater the risk that residual hydrogen sulfide compounds in the lees will be converted into mercaptans. So the first racking should not be delayed unnecessarily. I always look forward to the first racking because it is the first opportunity to speculate on the ultimate quality. Although the wine will be very yeasty and will not peak for another two years or so, you will at least get a sense of the depth of the flavor.

The purpose of this and subsequent rackings is to hasten clarification so that the wine can be bottled and corked as quickly as possible. Some of the impurities will be left behind at each racking, either settled on the bottom or clinging to the glass. After each racking there will be less sediment to go back into suspension when the barometric pressure falls, when the temperature rises or when the carboy gets disturbed. After two or three rackings over the next several months, the wine will be clear and ready for bottling.

The concern when racking is AIR. Until now, air has not been a factor because the wine has been in a carboy and capped either with an air lock or a stopper. It has also been saturated with carbon dioxide, which makes it less sensitive to air. But from now on, air will be the number one enemy. White wines are particularly delicate and suffer from any air contact. Each racking exposes it to more air and deprives it of a bit of its potential.

The number of rackings can be minimized by combining as many treatments and adjustments as possible at each racking. Add meta, oak chips, fining agents, adjust acid, adjust residual sugar, etc., all at the same racking, to the maximum extent possible. In addition to minimizing rackings, the rackings should take place as early as possible in the life of the wine. A wine will recover from a racking more readily when it is only a few weeks old than when it is a year old, by which time it will be considerably more delicate.

Treatments at first racking

The first racking will involve fining with Sparkolloid (or bentonite), adjusting total acid if necessary, and raising the level of residual sugar slightly, as well as adding meta at the rate of $1/4$ tsp. per 5 gallons. These steps are discussed separately in the next few sections but everything will be done at the same time when the wine is actually racked.

Testing and adjusting acidity

Total acid should be tested before racking in case a correction is needed. A correction may have been made before fermentation, but the acidity will have dropped somewhat during fermentation and cold stabilization. Hopefully, a careful titration will indicate total acidity to be in the ideal range of .60 –.70%. If it is less than .55%, the acid level should be raised to .55 –.60% at this time by one of the methods discussed in Chapter 8. If it is more than .75 – .80%, a correction should be made now if you want a dry white table wine. See Chapter 9. If a semi–sweet wine is the goal, the higher acid could be countered with higher residual sugar. If in doubt about your reading, do another titration test to avoid over–correcting.

Adjusting residual sugar

You will also want to add a little cane or beet sugar at this racking to sweeten the wine slightly. As discussed in the preceding chapter, the amount is strictly personal as it depends in good measure on your personal preference and the grape type. But let's assume that you like your white wines fairly dry and that total acidity tests at .65%. If a Clinitest indicates that residual sugar is approximately .05% and you have decided in favor of a final level of .65%, residual sugar will need to be raised by approximately .60%. With 640 ounces of wine in a 5–gallon carboy, you would want to add 3.8 ounces of sugar (640 x .006). Weigh it out and dissolve it in a small volume of hot water. Once it has cooled, add $1/4$ tsp. of meta to the sugar solution. If the acid level needs to be adjusted, the acid or potassium carbonate can also be dissolved in the sugar solution.

No, the added sugar will not start fermenting! Since the wine is relatively clear, most of the yeast cells and nutrients will have settled out. More nutrients will be eliminated at this racking with the Sparkolloid. The high alcohol content and the sulfite make the environment even more hostile. With almost no oxygen in the wine, the yeast colonies have little chance to re–establish. Be sure to keep it as cool as possible until it has clarified further. If the wine were at room temperature, fermentation probably would start again.

Making a Sparkolloid slurry

Sparkolloid is a very effective fining agent and will have no deleterious effect on the wine. You will probably not be able get a white wine totally clear without using Sparkolloid (or bentonite). Sparkolloid has to be prepared in the form of a hot slurry before use. Since the slurry should be added while piping hot, everything should be all set up and ready for racking before the slurry is prepared. I.e., the receiving carboys should be cleaned and ready. The sugar–meta–acid solution should be prepared and added to the empty carboys. I usually add $1/4$ to $1/2$ tsp. of tannin per carboy now, unless it was previously added. But tannin is optional, particularly if oak chips will be added.

Racking should be done outside or in the garage rather than bringing the wine inside. If the wine were to warm up, some of the precipitated tartrate crystals would immediately go back into suspension, and the wine would get cloudier. If the carboys have not been resting on a bench or counter, gently move them to an elevated position. The move will disturb the lees, but the wine will quickly clear again. Gently tip the carboy and insert a stick under one edge of the bottom. The wedge creates a deeper spot in the carboy, and that is where the racking stem will be positioned.

Now you are ready to proceed with making the Sparkolloid slurry. The normal dosage is 1 tsp. per gallon. Make the slurry by adding 5 tsp. of Sparkolloid to approximately $1^{1}/_{2}$ cups of boiling water. Don't use wine as it will scorch. Boil it for 25 minutes, stirring constantly and occasionally adding more water to maintain the original volume. After 25 minutes, it will be fully hydrated and you can proceed with racking. Don't let the slurry cool; it should be added piping hot while racking.

Basic racking procedure

Position the racking stem at the deepest point in the full carboy, hose attached, and draw up enough wine to fill the hose. Quickly cover the hose with your thumb and lower it into the empty carboy below. The bottom of the hose should be submerged so as to

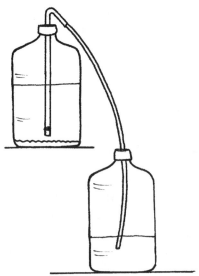

ILLUSTRATION C-1: Racking—no aeration

minimize splashing and aeration. *Illustration C-1.* With the aid of a funnel, add the Sparkolloid slurry in small doses at several times while racking. Rock and swirl the carboy to mix it in. Watch the upper carboy and when it is almost empty, lift the racking stem to avoid siphoning sediment along with the wine.

One caveat if you have small carboys, jugs or bottles left over from the previous racking — these must be blended into the main wine at this racking because the wine would not store safely in them for another two months. Before racking the carboys, any smaller containers should first be racked or poured into the new carboy.

With a little experience you will become quite adept at estimating volumes to get all containers full. In general, keep using smaller and smaller containers for the excess volume, and top the smallest one with water or comparable wine to fill it.

Needless to say, the carboys should be kept full at *all* times after fermentation is complete. This seems too fundamental to mention, but I have seen many otherwise good wines ruined by long–term aging with too much air space in the carboy. It is even more critical that smaller containers, such as jugs, be kept full and tightly stoppered, as wine cannot be safely kept in them for more than a few

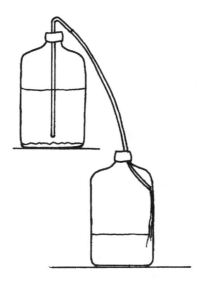

ILLUSTRATION C-2: Racking with aeration

weeks under the best of conditions.

Trapped CO_2 will continue to effervesce for a few minutes after the racking. After the small bubbles stop, plug the carboy once again with a solid rubber stopper wrapped with sticky plastic wrap and cap it with a fruit jar. Leave it outside or in a cool location until the next racking in about two months. An old refrigerator would work well but only holds one carboy; a walk–in cooler is great for cold stabilizing. Continue the stopper vigil, particularly if you had previous problems with H_2S. If it keeps popping out, microbes are converting the H_2S into mercaptans or, worse yet, into disulfides. *Appendix B.*

You will soon know whether Sparkolloid worked. In most cases the wine will appear to be totally clear in about ten days. If so, no more fining agents will be needed; only more time and another racking or two. Remember that no matter how clear the wine might look, it will always contain minute particles of Sparkolloid still in suspension. If you doubt this, shine a flashlight beam through it at night and you will see haze. This will eventually precipitate but it will take several weeks or months to achieve total clarity. In fact, it might not precipitate until the temperature warms. Having learned to tolerate a bit of sediment in my wines, I usually bottle early rather than waiting for total clarity, which may never arrive anyway.

Adding oak chips

If you want to add oak chips, the best time to do so is about two weeks after the first racking. By then most of the Sparkolloid will already have precipitated and will not coat the chips as they become waterlogged and sink. Five gallons of white wine will safely accommodate up to $1^1/_2$ cups of oak chips, shavings or splinters, as opposed to granular oak or toasted oak. Just stuff the chips in; if they produce effervescence, put an air lock back on temporarily. *See Chapter 14 for more details on oak additives.*

One could wait until the second racking to add oak, but by adding it at this earlier time, the wine will pick up a bit of tannin in case it needs to be fined with gelatin or isinglass at the second racking. The tannin will also help precipitate the residual Sparkolloid haze. The wine should left undisturbed in a cool location for another six to eight weeks while it continues to clear.

Fining Agents Glossary

Many different fining agents have been used over the years to clarify white and rosé wines, and they all have advantages and disadvantages. The short list that follows includes those that are usually effective and cause little or no loss in wine quality. All of them are Generally Recognized As Safe (GRAS) by the Food and Drug Administration, meaning that there is no upper limit as to amounts — from a safety point of view. Your wine supply shop may carry others as well. Note that a fining agent can generally be pre–mixed with other additives, such as meta or acid, but a fining agent should not be pre–mixed with another fining agent or with tannin.

It is best to experiment with test trials before using a fining agent to determine the optimum dosage. With Sparkolloid, for instance, try one at the rate of $1/2$ tsp. per gallon and others at $3/4$ tsp., 1 tsp. and $11/4$ tsp. per gallon. Additional saccharometer tubes can be used to do this. See which tubes are clearest the next morning. You are trying to find the point at which more of the fining agent fails to produce a clearer wine. To be honest, I usually just use 1 tsp. per gallon in the case of Sparkolloid.

SPARKOLLOID. 1 tsp. per gallon. Sparkolloid is effective in clarifying white wines and does not affect quality. The main disadvantage of Sparkolloid is that it's lees are very fluffy after settling and a disappointing volume of wine is lost. However, after it has settled for a week or two, 2 tablespoons of isinglass can be gently stirred in without racking. It will settle on top of the Sparkolloid and compact it slightly, so it will be less easily stirred up. Topping with bentonite would accomplish the same goal, but bentonite will not clear very well unless the wine is brought to room temperature. Another disadvantage of Sparkolloid is that it takes several months for all of the residual Sparkolloid to precipitate. These are significant disadvantages, but if you want a clear white wine, Sparkolloid is the most dependable in my experience.

BENTONITE. 1 tsp. = 5.4 g. Like Sparkolloid, bentonite also attracts positively–charged particles. It can be as effective as Sparkolloid and is equally benign. Rarely can a white wine be totally cleared without using one or the other. The principal disadvantage of bentonite is that it is most effective if the wine is at room temperature when racked and then kept warm until the next racking in 10 to 14 days. If the wine is chilled, some of the bentonite will go back into suspension. Use of bentonite would throw off the sequence of racking and clarifying outlined in Chapter Two because the wine should not be sweetened at the first racking if it will be kept warm afterwards — renewed fermentation is likely. In other words, use of bentonite would probably require one additional racking. It would also mean additional moving of heavy carboys unless you are fortunate enough to have a heated garage or room to use for winemaking.

Bear in mind that the sequence of clarification steps can be altered once the gross lees have settled out. Some winemakers wait until early summer to fine with bentonite. By this time, the wine is warmer and clearer, so a smaller dosage can be used with good results.

A hot slurry is prepared and added in the same manner as Sparkolloid. Again, it would be best to experiment with some test trials to find the best dosage. Otherwise, try a dosage of 2 tsp. per 5 gallons if fining right after the gross less have settled; or 1 tsp. if fining in late spring or early summer when the wine is almost clear.

AGGLOMERATED BENTONITE. 2 g./gal.; 1 tsp. = 3.7 g. It is much easier to make a slurry with bentonite that is in agglomerated or prilled form. KWK and Vitaben are two brands. Just add a teaspoon or two to a cup of warm water, let it soak overnight and it will be ready the next day. Agglomerated bentonite is more compact than regular bentonite after settling, so less wine is sacrificed. Note that bentonite should not be used on red wines as it takes out part of the color. Also, bentonite and Sparkolloid have such a high affinity for proteins that they will strip out pectic enzyme added at the same time — add the enzyme later.

BEERMAKER'S ISINGLASS. This protein is an effective and benign fining agent for either white and rosé wines. It could be tried in lieu of Sparkolloid or bentonite and might be the only fining agent needed. It attracts negatively–charged particles but needs the presence of a small amount of tannin for flocculation and maximum effectiveness. The tannin from any oak chips that were added will normally suffice. If oak was not added, the isinglass can be preceded or followed up with $1/4$ to $1/2$ tsp. of tannin per 5 gallons. Four ounce bottles of isinglass are available at beermaking supply stores.

GELATIN. $1/8$ to $1/2$ g./gal.; 3.0 g./tsp. Like isinglass, gelatin has a protein base and attracts negatively–charged particles. However, it is more difficult to work with because it requires more tannin than isinglass to flocculate. If you can't run test trials to determine the right gelatin–to–tannin ratio for the white wine in question, precede or follow the gelatin with an equal *weight* of tannin. Special grades of gelatin for winemaking are available, but Knox unflavored gelatin seems to work just as well. Keep notes on the amount added.

Gelatin can also be used in red wines at the rate of $1/2$ –1 tsp. per 5 gallons to remove excess tannin and soften it before bottling. Prepare by dissolving in a small volume of warm water and letting it soak overnight.

Chapter Five

SUBSEQUENT RACKINGS

he purpose of the second racking is to separate the wine from the very fluffy Sparkolloid lees that have settled and to make a further acid adjustment, if necessary. Meta is not necessary but the wine would accommodate another ⅛ tsp. meta per 5 gallons if you are so inclined. If the acid reading is close to what it should be, I would avoid the temptation to tinker further. If total acidity is .60%, and perhaps even as low as .55%, leave well enough alone. But if a careful titration indicates that the acidity is less than .55%, this is the time to adjust it.

How much tartaric acid to add? There are no hard–and–fast rules governing this topic, and opinions will differ. I try to avoid raising total acidity by more than +.1% with artificial acid because it tends to be harsh and show through in the long run. On the other hand, I prefer to bottle with acidity of .60% and absolutely will not bottle with acidity of less than .55%. Accordingly, if total acid is between .50% and .60%, I add enough tartaric acid to raise total acidity to .60%. If it is between .45% and .50%, I use enough to raise it by +.1%. If it is less than .45%, I add enough to raise it to .55%, regardless of how much is required to reach that level.

If acidity is above .75 –.80%, you have the option of either adding more sugar to balance the excess acidity or of lowering acidity. If it is close to .75%, I would be inclined to rely on additional sugar. If it is well above .8%, it should either be blended or lowered artificially by one of the methods described in Chapter 9, perhaps in combination with a higher level of RS.

Note that Clinitest tablets will not yet accurately measure residual sugar. It takes several weeks for the cane or beet sugar added at the first racking to convert to glucose and fructose. Clinitest will not work on sucrose.

The second racking will normally take place about two months after the first racking. If the sugar–acid balance seems right to my palate and the wine is crystal clear, I sometimes skip the second racking and let it cold stabilize for 4 or 5 months on the Sparkolloid lees. The wine can then be bottled directly out of the carboy. As explained in Chapter 7, the necessary sulfite can be added by dissolving the meta in 25 ml of water and dispensing 1 ml into each bottle with a pipet. However, if the wine is not totally clear, I will rack a second time, maybe using a second fining agent.

Second fining agent

In most cases after fining with Sparkolloid, the wine will appear to be totally clear after two months of settling and further cold stabilizing. If not, you might want to use another fining agent at the second racking. Ideally, a series of lab tests would be conducted to determine the optimum combination and concentration of fining agents. But that's not a very practical option for a home winemaker fermenting small lots. With only 5 to 10 gallons, it is more practical simply to try another fining agent if the first one was not completely successful. If the second fining agent is not successful, then resort to an option not available to the commercial vintner — bottling with a little haze!

A number of different fining agents could be used for the second attempt, but beermaker's isinglass has come to be my choice. It is very gentle and even if it does not prove to be the complete answer, a small dose will settle without affecting quality or causing a major setback in the quest for clarity. If the wine is nearly clear, 1 or 2 teaspoons of the liquid beermaker's isinglass per 5 gallons might be adequate. The bit of tannin which was previously added or which leached out of the oak chips will promote flocculation of the isinglass. Follow the same basic racking procedure as in the first racking, adding the isinglass while racking. Continue storing in a cool spot until the next racking.

Gelatin could be used rather than isinglass, but gelatin requires the presence of more tannin to flocculate and is generally more difficult to work with. Whereas the Sparkolloid attracted negatively charged particles, both isinglass and gelatin have protein bases and attract positively–charged particles in suspension. Kieselsol (.5-1.0 ml/gal.) can be used in lieu of tannin to precipitate gelatin.

Bentonite is another good fining agent, but will not precipitate until the temperature of the wine gets into the 60's. If you want to use bentonite, it might be better to wait until late spring or early summer to do so. The wine will be clearer by then and less will be needed — maybe only 1 tsp. per carboy, made into a slurry in the same manner as Sparkolloid.

Third racking

The purpose of this racking is to add $\frac{1}{4}$ tsp. of meta in anticipation of bottling in 3 to 4 weeks. The wine will be quite clear by now, hopefully brilliant. If not, plan to bottle anyway as the remaining haze will not affect the flavor. It will eventually precipitate and can be decanted off when the bottle is opened for consumption.

As discussed in Chapter 7, if the wine is clear enough, this racking could be bypassed and the wine bottled at this point. The 50 ppm of meta which the wine needs at bottling can be added by dissolving 1/4 tsp. in 25 ml of water and dispensing 1 ml into each bottle.

Chapter Six

FERMENTING RED TABLE WINES

he procedure for fermenting red grapes is less involved in some respects than for whites. Clarification is not the challenge it is with whites, and red wines are not as sensitive to air contact. In this sense, the process is easier for red wines than whites. Note that I did not say it is easier to make a great red wine than white, because that is not the case.

The general procedure is as follows:
1. The stems are separated and discarded at crushing.
2. The crushed grapes are fermented on the skins in an open container for several days before being pressed. The "cap" of emaciated skins is punched down at least twice daily.
3. When unfermented sugar has dropped to approximately 0° Brix, the wine is pressed and fermentation is completed in a carboy topped with an air lock.
4. Red wines should be fermented warmer than whites — 70 to 85° is the preferred range. A higher fermenting temperature is not mandatory, but more flavor and complexity will be extracted if it is.

A workshop or spare room with temperature control is an ideal place to ferment red wines.

Preparatory

The procedures in Chapter Two for culling out bad fruit, cleanliness and preparation of a yeast starter solution are equally applicable to red grapes. If any of the clusters are hard and raisined, discard them.

Crushing and de-stemming

Since the stems must be separated before fermentation to avoid extreme astringency in the finished wine, it is a great convenience, if not a necessity, to own or have access to a crusher–stemmer. A crusher–stemmer automatically separates the stems while it crushes. *Illustration D.* Without a crusher–stemmer, at least 90% of

ILLUSTRATION D

the stems will have to be raked out by hand after crushing and the remaining grapes stripped off. This can be done but it becomes extremely tedious with even as little as 100 pounds. If you don't own a crusher–stemmer, try to borrow or rent one for a few hours.

After the grapes are crushed and de–stemmed, the mass goes into a primary fermenter, which for most home winemakers will consist of a large plastic garbage can or barrel with a lid. I have several different sizes of the Rubbermaid® Brute® containers with lids and find them to be quite satisfactory. The primary fermenter should be filled to no more than 3/4 of capacity to allow room for the cap of grape skins, or *chapeau*, which will rise to the surface as fermentation starts. A normal dose of meta should be added when crushing. Although the meta is not necessary in that red grapes have an abundance of tannin, which by itself is a good preservative, the meta is nevertheless desirable because it kills the malolactic bacteria which might otherwise multiply and establish. There are three strains of malolactic bacteria, two of which are undesirable. If malolactic fermentation is desired, the better procedure is to kill all natural bacteria with meta and add a cultured strain later. In addition, I normally add pectic enzyme at crushing in the belief that it hastens the breakdown of the berry and extraction of flavors.

Testing sugar, acidity and pH

Fermentable sugar should be a little higher in red grapes than white — 22° to 24° Brix on the saccharometer is ideal. Many fine red wines have been made with higher or lower sugar readings, however. Be sure to get an accurate titration of total acid. The juice is clear right after crushing but picks up pigment from the skins soon after fermentation starts, making it difficult to read the endpoint when titrating with phenolphthalein. Total acidity should be between .65% and 1.0%, at the time of the crush. It will drop somewhat during fermentation and cold stabilization, probably .05–.10%. If the acidity is close to 1.0%, you will probably want to consider malolactic fermentation as a means of getting it down into the desired range for a finished red wine — .55% to .70%.

Winemakers always want to know the pH of their red wine musts. And for good reason, as it exceeds acidity in importance.

The pH, or power hydrogen ion, is a measure of the concentration of hydrogen ions in solution and is basically a measure of the strength of the acidity. The pH of musts should be between 3.2 and 3.6, with the lower figure being more acidic and sour. A pH of 3.5 would be preferable to 3.2 or 3.3 for a finished red wine. Wines with a pH much higher than 3.6 will be unstable and have a shorter shelf life. And wines with a pH below 3.2 will be too sour. So 3.2 to 3.6 is the preferred pH range.

Important as the pH of a red wine may be, it is somewhat academic for the home winemaker, who usually has no control as to when the grapes are picked. And although acid corrections will also affect pH, corrections should be made based on total acid, not pH. So if you do not have access to a pH meter, proceed on the assumption that if the acidity and sugar are in the right range, the pH will be also.

Adjusting acidity

The desired acid range for a finished red wine is a little lower than for whites. Total acid in a finished red wine should be approximately .60% – .65%, possibly even as low as .55%, and not more than .70%. Total acidity will, of course, be higher before fermentation.

If total acid of the must is in the range of .65 –1.0%, it will not need to be corrected before fermentation and perhaps not ever. Total acid will normally drop by .05 – .10% or more during fermentation and cold stabilization — this can be expected as a natural part of the process. Malolactic fermentation would lower it by at least .15%, and perhaps by as much as .40%, depending on how much of the total acidity was originally comprised of malic acid. If malolactic fermentation pushes acidity below .55%, it can be raised by adding tartaric acid.

Similarly, if the must acidity is less than .70%, I would use meta at crushing and press and cool the wine when unfermented sugar has dropped to 0° Brix — to discourage malolactic fermentation, which might lower acidity too much. If the acidity of the must is much below .60% at the crush, raise it to .60% or .65% before fermentation and use meta to discourage MLF.

If the acidity of the must is above 1.0%, lower it to that level chemically with calcium carbonate and plan to put it through malolactic fermentation as well. Note that when a must is extremely acidic, the pH is likely to be too low to support MLF. Lowering total acidity to 1.0% before fermentation will probably raise the pH to the minimum level needed to sustain malolactic fermentation, which is about 3.2 in a red wine for most strains of ML bacteria. See Chapter 9. In addition, yeast extract should be added as a nutrient for the ML bacteria if the acid is quite high.

Inoculating and fermenting

When the yeast starter is foamy and active, sprinkle it over the surface of the must without stirring it in. If the must is held at 75 – 80°, fermentation should start in a few hours and will be indicated at first by small, foamy bubbles. After a day, a cap of crushed grapes and skins will be visible. After about two days the cap will rise high, indicating that it is time to add the ML starter and yeast extract if MLF is planned.

Controlling fermentation

There is little that can be done to slow the rate of fermentation of a red must being fermented at higher temperatures. Even a slower yeast, such as Epernay 2, will naturally be very active in the desired temperature range of 70–85°. No matter what the yeast strain, sugar Brix is likely to drop 10 – 15° within 48 hours after becoming active. You could ferment cooler in order to prolong the fermentation and skin–contact period, but that would be counterproductive as less flavor is extracted at lower temperatures.

For most red wines, it is best to forget about the length of the fermentation period. Keep the temperature in the 70 – 85° range and plan to press when the sugar drops to 0°. This will result in a wine with good structure and complexity and one which will not take years and years to mature. If you are intent on making a "big" wine, see the section on extended maceration in Chapter 11.

Punching down the cap

The cap has to be punched down at least twice a day during fermentation — i.e., pushed under the surface and covered with liquid. The object of punching down is to prevent aerobic bacteria from developing on the cap and also to promote contact between the wine and skins. Commercial wineries pump juice from the bottom of the tank and spray it over the cap. The home winemaker has to do it the old fashioned way of punching down.

Almost any flat surface can be used to push it down, such as a stainless steel sauce pan or the bottom of a plastic pail. Care should always be taken not to expose fermenting wines to metals other than stainless steel. Non–resinous wood, plastic and stainless steel are all acceptable. After punching down, the utensils should be removed from the room and washed to avoid attracting fruit flies.

If your grapes had a very high Brix and you are concerned that the level of alcohol might end up too high, the alcohol can be kept slightly lower by fermenting warmer (80–85°) and punching down more frequently and vigorously. This lets more of the alcohol evaporate.

Be alert throughout fermentation for potential problems with hydrogen sulfide. Rotten egg stink requires immediate remedial action. I keep mentioning this unpleasant possibility not because it is so common, but because it is so much easier to correct if dealt with promptly. *Appendix B.*

Pressing

When the saccharometer indicates that the unfermented sugar is around 0° B., fermentation will have slowed to nearly a standstill. This will usually be 5 or 6 days after fermentation started. The grapes will be quite emaciated, and the cap will not reform as quickly or rise as high. It's time to press! You could press sooner if the goal is a lighter wine, but it should not be allowed to drop much below 0° Brix because fermentation might stick if it is racked and pressed with too little unfermented sugar remaining. Even at 0° Brix, about 2% sugar remains. The saccharometer is not accurate because the high alcohol level has altered the specific density of the liquid.

Dip everything out of the primary fermenter, pour it into the press basket and press in the same manner as white grapes. The hard–pressed portion will have more tannin and be less fruity than the free run, so some winemakers keep the two portions separate and blend them later. Or not, as seems best.

Carboy fermentation

After pressing, the wine goes into clean carboys which are topped with an air lock. Fill the carboys to the top and let the wine ferment to total dryness at approximately 70°. Excess volumes can be fermented to dryness in gallon jugs or even in wine bottles if you have an extra small air lock stopper. The small containers could be used first for topping up at the first racking. Continue to monitor for rotten egg smell.

First racking

The remainder of this chapter assumes that malolactic fermentation is not desired; if it is, skip the meta and refer to Chapter 12.

After Clinitest confirms that a red wine is totally dry, it should be racked, sulfited ($1/4$ tsp./5 gal.) and chilled. Some wines will ferment below .1% on the Clinitest scale and others will "stick" at .3%, which is the same for all practical purposes as .1%. A red wine should not be left on the lees at higher temperatures any longer than necessary, due to the risk of unwanted side reactions and the tendency of volatile acids to increase. If I had no problems with H_2S, I usually let the gross lees settle for about one month and then rack and sulfite. But if I encountered H_2S, I rack and sulfite immediately after Clinitest tells me it is dry. It is always best to lower the temperature as soon as the wine is dry (unless MLF is sought).

Unlike white wines, which suffer from exposure to air, red wines will benefit from a little air contact immediately after fermentation stops. Trickle it down the sides of the carboy at the first racking to aerate it slightly. See *Illustration C-2*, page 47.

If you had problems with H_2S during fermentation, a bit of copper should be added after fermentation is over. The preferred method is to use a dilute solution of copper sulfate (1% $CuSO_4 \bullet 5H_2O$) because you know exactly how much copper is being added. I would add either .1 ppm or .2 ppm of copper. To add .1 ppm of copper, add .15 ml of copper sulfate per gallon. The FDA limit for residual copper is .2 ppm, so either quantity will be safe. If copper sulfate is not readily available, trickle the wine down some copper wires while racking, as shown in the illustration page 140. This adds a few parts per million of copper which likewise helps neutralize the sulfide compounds.

For the reason discussed in Chapter 2 on white wines, a solid stopper should be substituted for the air lock. This is the easiest way to find out whether microbes are converting the residual sulfur compounds into mercaptans. See *Appendix B*.

Subsequent rackings

After a month or two, more of the gross lees will have settled, and the wine should be racked again. No more meta will be needed until right before bottling. This time, however, and at all future rackings, the end of the racking hose should be submerged to minimize aeration. *Illustration C-1*, page 46. With red wines you need not go to the extreme of displacing the air in the new carboy with inert gas before racking, but don't unnecessarily expose it to air. It is sufficient to limit the number of rackings and keep the end of the racking tube below the wine level as it is being racked.

Subsequent rackings should take place at 3 to 4 month intervals and the wine bottled between late spring and early fall. I like to age red wines in carboys through one summer and bottle in September, just before the new crop arrives. A fair amount of solids will precipitate as the temperature warms during the summer, which means less sediment in the bottle.

Some winemakers age their red wines in carboys for two years or more before bottling. This is also acceptable. Whether extended carboy aging is beneficial depends on the effect of air contact when the wine is bottled at a more mature age, which is anyone's guess. My preference is to bottle earlier so as to free up the carboys for the new crop.

Final racking

About a month before bottling, the wine should be racked for the last time. Add $1/4 - 3/8$ tsp. of meta per 5 gallons. Meta is recommended to rule out malolactic fermentation after bottling and to prolong shelf life. Some winemakers would argue that $3/8$ tsp. is too much meta, as it will leave a sulfite odor immediately after bottling. However, the sulfite odor will disappear in two or three months and your wine will age better. If $3/8$ tsp. seems like too much to you, use only $1/4$ tsp. You could also fine with $1/2$ to 1 tsp. of gelatin per carboy if the wine seems overly tannic and needs to be softened. But give the gelatin a few weeks to settle out before bottling. See Chapter 7 for comments on bottling.

Chapter Seven

BOTTLING

 bottling party can be a lot of fun, particularly if livened with samples of prior vintages. But it also involves a great deal of preparation, tedious work and clean up. Bottles have to be rinsed and sulfited, wine racked into them and corked and everything cleaned up afterwards. This is undoubtedly the reason so many homemade wines get bottled later, rather than sooner.

I always bottle in traditional wine bottles, but there are other alternatives. The most expedient container would be a 22–ounce beer bottle capped with a crown cap. It will not impress anyone, but the wine will keep every bit as well as with a traditional bottle and cork. I know one gentleman who uses sparkling cider bottles and a plastic mushroom cap as a closure. A lever device is available which pries the cap off. He saves the plastic caps, boils them to resize and uses them several times. Crown caps would seem more expedient than mushroom caps, but every winemaker develops his own preferences.

Most people will think in terms of conventional wine bottles. New wine bottles can be purchased at wine supply stores but the cost mounts quickly if you have much wine. It's a question of how much wine you have and what your time is worth. If you have the time, it's easy to find used bottles at the recycle depot or to get a restaurant to save them for you. The labels can be soaked and scraped off in a hot solution of soap or trisodium phosphate. A spray washer which attaches to an outdoor or laundry sink tap makes rinsing more convenient.

All wines should be bottled with a low level of free SO_2 in solution, added shortly before bottling. The obvious method is to add sulfite (1/4 tsp./5 gal. for reds, slightly less for whites) while racking the finished wine into a clean carboy. The wine can then be racked out of that carboy into the bottles. But this involves two exposures to air. Here's a bottling procedure that eliminates one exposure. I've used it for many years with good results.

After the wine has cleared to your satisfaction and about three or four weeks before you plan to bottle, rack the wine for the last time, making any last minute adjustments to residual sugar and acidity, adding meta as described. Any particulate from the sugar addition will settle out during the next two or three weeks. You can then rack directly out of the carboy into the bottles. Here's the twist. Before bottling, rinse the empty bottles with a highly concentrated sulfite solution (1 tbs./qt.) and drain thoroughly. The sulfite solution that clings to the bottle will boost the level of free sulfite slightly for good shelf life. Pour a few ounces of the concentrated solution from one bottle to the next with the aid of a funnel. Discard the used solution every few bottles and start with fresh as it tends to pick up lint and dust going from bottle to bottle.

Another good technique, when a white wine clears with Sparkolloid and has the right residual sugar–acid balance after the first adjustment, is to dissolve 1/4 tsp. of meta in 25 ml of water and dispense 1 ml into each bottle with a pipet. Then rack directly into the bottles. This will result in the very minimum of exposures to air — only the first racking plus the bottling:

- Wine falls still.
- Cold stabilize — 1 to 2 months.
- First racking — add sulfite, fine with Sparkolloid, adjust sugar and acid, etc.
- Stabilize — 3 to 5 months at room temperature.
- Add 1 ml of sulfite solution per bottle and bottle direct out of carboy.

White wines are not so delicate that you need to go to such lengths to minimize air contact. On the other hand, since it does no harm to clarify for several months on the Sparkolloid lees, there is no compelling reason to rack more.

When filling the bottles, leave room for only the cork and ½ inch of air space. You'll need a clip near the end of your $5/16$" siphoning hose to cut off the wine flow, or else a bottling stem with a cutoff valve. The bottom of the hose should be at the bottom of the wine bottle to minimize splashing and aeration. The wine displaces/absorbs the sulfite atmosphere as the bottle fills, and damage from air contact is minimized this way.

Dip the corks in warm water for a few seconds to lubricate them slightly; sulfite is optional. Don't soak them for more than a minute or so as they get mushy and tend to ooze back out of the bottle. After corking, stand the bottles upright for a few hours to let the air pressure in the bottle equalize with the atmosphere.

If you plan to cellar your wine for several years, use of a sealing cap might help keep the cork from drying out. But this is disputed. The humidity in your cellar is certainly the more important consideration. Store the bottles neck down or flat, so the cork does not dry out. The ideal cellar would have high humidity, a constant temperature of 55°, and no light or vibrations. Labels, if you use them, are best affixed with a glue stick. I usually stack bottles destined for personal consumption in bins without labels to save time. If I later want to give away or trade wines, I add labels then.

After two months in the bottle, the wine will have recovered from "bottling shock", and you will have your best impression yet of the finished product. A white wine with good acid will continue to improve for another two years and a red wine for three or four years. Even a disappointing wine will improve for six to twelve months after bottling, so bottle it even if it seems like a waste of time.

April or May is a good time to bottle a white wine because it is as clear as you are likely to get it, and it will still be relatively cool. But, again, if your wine is clear in March, don't wait to bottle — the sooner, the better! Red wines could be bottled in May but less bottle sediment will develop if they are carboy–aged through one summer.

Bottling Glossary

PLASTIC BOTTLING STEM. Many home winemakers use a plastic bottling stem affixed to the end of the racking hose. The one I am familiar with fits both 5/16" and 3/8" hoses. Wine flows when the valve on the bottom is pushed against the bottle. Fill it to the very top and when the filler is removed, the wine drops to just the right level. A 5/16" hose and plastic clip to cut off wine flow also works well for filling bottles.

BOTTLE WASHER. This is a faucet spray which screws onto an outdoor or laundry sink tap. It is convenient for rinsing a large number of bottles but not a necessity. I've read that they can damage the water pipes under your house (the abrupt cutoff) but have never experienced that problem.

CORKER. The type that compresses the entire length of the cork before it gets rammed into the bottle is preferable to the tunnel type, which scrapes off bits of cork as it is forced through the orifice into the bottle. Bench or floor models are more convenient but considerably more expensive. The hand held type is adequate for small quantities. Be sure to try the model under consideration if you intend to use synthetic corks.

CORKS. The typical domestic 750 ml bottle uses a no. 9 cork. Some imported bottles have a slightly narrower neck in which the less expensive no. 8's work better. I doubt if the wine keeps any better using 1³/₄" corks, as opposed to 1¹/₂", but some people think it does. And I doubt if plastic caps do much to keep the corks from drying out, since humidity of the cellar is the big factor. But plastic caps do add a nice aesthetic touch.

SYNTHETIC CORKS. Synthetic corks have many practical advantages for the home winemaker. They will not taint the wine or dry out and let air in, so you should never have a "corked" bottle of wine. Since synthetic corks are chemically inert, bottled wine can be stored upright to allow the haze to settle on the bottom before decanting and consuming. Since they are so difficult to insert, they are also very difficult to remove and can be taken on a plane or shipped with no concern about leakage. The brand I am familiar with, SupremeCorq, comes in many different colors, and the colors can be used as a basis for sorting different batches of wine without having to label them.

The principal disadvantage is that they inhibit the normal aging of the wine. A wine closed with a thermoplastic cork will take two and a half or three years to develop the bouquet and flavor that it would otherwise have at 6 to 12 months. Perhaps this only means that thermoplastic corks will preserve a wine longer and that ultimately the wines will have plenty of bouquet and flavor. After three years in the bottle, they seem to have a richer flavor than would be expected but still lack bouquet. Maybe in 5-6 years they will have flavor and bouquet in abundance, it's too soon to tell. If your time frame is two to three years, you might be more satisfied with natural corks.

Another major drawback is that these corks are very difficult to insert. They re-form *very* quickly after being released from the constriction of the corker and seal against the neck of the bottle. Air cannot escape as the cork is pushed further into the bottle. The air pressure builds up and makes it difficult to insert them all the way. (The positive air pressure may also be related to the slowness of bouquet to develop). The manufacturer says that this problem of pressure build up can be countered by bottling with a piece of 20-pound fishing line in the neck and pulling it out after the cork is in place, something I have not tried.

Chapter Eight

RAISING ACIDITY

s grapes ripen, the sugar content rises and total acid falls. The amount of tartaric acid remains fairly constant throughout the life of the grape; it is other acids — principally malic — that decrease. Grapes grown in hot climates can quickly pass their peak and end up with too little acid and too much sugar. Corrective measures are sometimes needed to bring the acid up to the minimum desired pre–fermentation level of .60 –.65%.

Blending

Blending should be one of the first options to be considered. The natural acids in another wine or must are always to be preferred over manufactured acids, which will eventually taste harsh if added in any significant amount. If high–acid grapes are available, they can be blended with a low acid must. You could even blend in some of last year's high acid wine. This could be done after fermentation is complete. Better yet, blend it directly into the must at the peak of fermentation (sugar between 20° and 15° B.).

Never hesitate to blend any high–acid wine or must into any low–acid wine or must. Unusual blends of varieties can make delightful wines, and it's more fun to experiment than be stuck with a finished wine that is not balanced properly. The only caveat in blending is that only wines of sound quality should be used. Never use a wine tainted with odors or off flavors for blending or, contrary to what you might expect, you will usually end up with two batches of equally bad wine. If the wine to be blended has too much acid or suffers from a slight over–exposure to oak or sulfite, it will probably be acceptable for blending. But if it suffers from unpleasant organic flavors, such as ethyl acetate or acetaldehyde, even a small quantity will ruin a good wine. So always taste both lots before blending.

Following is an equation that will work for a quantitative blending, such as raising or lowering total acidity (or residual sugar).

$$TA_1 + TA_2\ X = TA_b\ (1 + X) \text{ where:}$$
TA_1 = Total acid wine no. 1
TA_2 = Total acid wine no. 2
TA_b = Desired total acid of blend
X = Ratio by volume of wine no. 2 to wine no. 1

If total acid of wine no. 1 is 1.3 and total acid of wine no. 2 is .55 and you want a blend having total acid of .8, then $X = 2$. The result is the *ratio*. In this case, two volumes of wine no. 2 is needed for one volume of wine no. 1 to end up with acidity of .8%.

Adding acid

Adding artificial acids is a common method of dealing with acid deficiency, used by commercial wineries as well as home winemakers. It's better to add the acid before fermentation as it will marry better with the natural grape compounds. In addition, a must with abnormally low acid is more inclined toward problems during fermentation. If total acid is less than .55%, an acid correction obviously will be needed. Raise it to .60% or .65% when you crush because it will drop slightly during fermentation and cold stabilization. Raising it to this level will not result in an over–correction.

Tartaric acid is normally preferred for raising acidity in either red or white musts. It is the dominant and most desirable of the three principal acids. It is also the safest acid to add in that some of it will precipitate as potassium bitartrate during cold stabilization in case you over–corrected. Adding 3.8 g. per gallon will raise acidity by .1%. but see the Glossary below.

Hopefully, acidity will end up in the desired range after fermentation. But if it is much less than .55 – .60% after fermentation, it should be raised to that level. Otherwise, the wine will taste "flabby," even if bottled drier, and will have shorter shelf life. But before making an adjustment, bring the wine to room temperature for a week or two. Some of the natural tartrate salts will go back into solution and raise total acidity slightly. Then test it again. The natural salts are better than articificial acids and if only a slight increase is needed after cold stabilization, just bringing the wine to room temperature for a few days might be all that is needed.

Be cautious when adding acid, and never add more than necessary. Raising the acidity of a finished wine by .1% with artificial acids is a significant correction which should be exceeded only when absolutely necessary. A wine to which more has been added might taste fine initially, but the acid addition will become increasingly harsh and noticeable as the wine ages. To avoid over–correcting, I usually add half the estimated amount, test it and add more at the next racking if necessary. It is also good practice to double check your reading before correcting.

Acids Glossary

TARTARIC ACID 3.8 g./gal. raises acidity by +.1%, but some will settle out during cold stabilization as potassium tartrate. It might have to be added a second time. 1 tsp. = 4.6 g. Tartaric acid is normally the best choice for treating acid–deficient grapes as it is the principal acid found in grapes as well as the most stable. A small quantity of this basic supply should be kept on hand.

MALIC ACID. 3.4 g./gallon raises acidity by +.1%; 1 tsp. = 4.0 g. As the grapes ripen, sugar goes up and acidity goes down; it is principally the malic acid that falls off. Malic acid is a good choice for raising the acidity of "hot–climate" white grapes of the fruity variety. It is slightly less sour and a little fresher than tartaric. Tartaric acid will lower the pH of a wine more; so if pH is too high and you want to lower it as much as possible, tartaric acid should be used rather than malic.

Note that only half of the artificial version of malic acid will be converted to lactic by malolactic fermentation; the other half remains as malic. This means that if any malic acid was added along the way, a chromatography test will no longer be valid. Ordinarily, of course, if acid is low to the point of needing to be increased, one would try to discourage MLF.

(CITRIC ACID). Citric acid is not an essential supply item. It can be safely added only after fermentation and only after malolactic fermentation. It should be avoided in red wine and used most sparingly in white wines. The overwhelming majority of the total acids in a wine consist of tartaric and malic; very little is citric and most wine drinkers would not appreciate a strong citric flavor in a wine. If you think a wine would benefit from a little citric acid, the better and safer choice woiuld be an acid blend.

(ACID BLEND). This is a mixture of tartaric, malic and citric acids which is more commonly used in adjusting acidity in fruit wines. The ratio of acids probably varies somewhat depending on the packager. It is comparable in strength to pure tartaric, but due to the presence of citric acid should be used only in white wines and only after fermentation and MLF are complete. If the acid level needs a significant increase, tartaric acid is again preferable.

Chapter Nine

LOWERING ACIDITY

owering acidity is not as easy as raising it. Ideally, only the malic or citric acid would be lowered and tartaric — the most stable and desirable of the principal acids — would not be affected. Unfortunately, most acid–reduction techniques neutralize all the tartaric acid before affecting any of the malic or citric acid. As a result, care must be taken not to eliminate too much of the tartaric, which would reduce the stability and shelf life of the wine and affect the flavor as well. Here are some options for correcting excess acidity:

Blending

This is again the safest and most conservative choice, if you have low–acid grapes or wine on hand. This will be the exception rather than the rule. So some other technique will normally have to be used.

Amelioration

The addition of water, known as "amelioration," to dilute the acid is a common practice in cool locales where the summers are not hot enough to fully ripen the grapes. One gallon of water added to 5 gallons of must reduces acidity by about 10%, taking into account the ability of an increased volume of liquid to hold more acid. Since it also dilutes the flavor, one–to–five is about as far as amelioration should be pushed.

It is usually a good idea to sweeten the water to about 20° Brix (about 2 pounds per gallon) before adding it. Grapes that are high in acid are probably low in sugar, and sweetening prevents the alcohol level from dropping too low. Although it is not a legal practice by commercial wineries in the United States, the practice of adding sugar (known as "chaptalization") is common in many countries where grapes have difficulty ripening.

Amelioration would not be my first choice as a means of lowering acid. But if the acid level of the must were well above the desired maximum of 1.0%, amelioration could be used in combination with some of the following alternatives.

Calcium carbonate

Calcium carbonate ($CaCO_3$), or precipitated chalk, is often used to lower the acid level in a must. It does not require cold stabilization to force complete precipitation, as does potassium carbonate. (In fact, it will not precipitate at low temperatures). However, calcium carbonate is more likely to affect the flavor than potassium carbonate and can take many months to precipitate. Due to the latter disadvantage, calcium carbonate is acceptable for reducing acidity in a must or perhaps in a very young wine but should never be used shortly before bottling.

Use calcium carbonate sparingly because it preferentially reduces tartaric acid. Not until all the tartaric acid has been neutralized will it act on the malic or citric acid. Add too much and you run the risk of reducing all the tartaric acid. For this reason, total acid should not be lowered by more than .3% or .4% using either calcium carbonate or potassium carbonate. If acidity needs to be lowered significantly, try adding all the $CaCO_3$ to a portion of the must — say one–fourth. The carbonate will reduce all the tartaric in this portion and part of the malic. Plenty of tartaric will remain after the other three–fourths is blended back in.

Adding 2.5 g./gallon will reduce acidity by roughly .1%, but this should be confirmed with test trials as the effect can vary. It will also raise the pH but by an amount that will vary greatly depending on the chemistry of the must. Since weights per teaspoon of this very fluffy compound vary considerably, it should be weighed rather than measured by volume.

Potassium carbonate 1 tsp. = 6.0 g.

Potassium carbonate (K_2CO_3) reduces acidity by converting tartaric acid to potassium bitartrate which can be precipitated out by chilling the wine for several weeks. Adding 3.8 g/gal. will reduce acidity by about .1%, although its effect cannot be predicted with great precision because you never know how completely it will precipitate. Sometimes it lowers acidity more than expected, apparently by initiating the tartrate precipitation process. So it is better to conduct test trials before using it. If you want to be conservative, add half of the estimated amount and test the acid level after two or three weeks of cold stabilization. If more is needed, the first addition serves as a guide for adding more of the chemical.

Again, total acid should not be lowered by more than .3 – .4% using K_2CO_3 to avoid the possibility of eliminating all the tartaric. And it should not be used in addition to calcium carbonate. Potassium carbonate will raise pH more than calcium carbonate.

Potassium bicarbonate ($KHCO_3$) is essentially the same as potassium carbonate. Use 3.4 grams per gallon to lower acidity by .1%.

Malolactic fermentation

As discussed in detail in Chapter 12, malolactic fermentation is a very effective way to lower acidity. It is unique in that it lowers malic acid without affecting tartaric. The disadvantage of malolactic fermentation is that the risk of spoilage is greater at the higher temperatures necessary to sustain the malolactic bacteria. And it reduces the fruitiness in the finished wine.

Cold stabilization

Super chilling a finished wine down to 25° F. for an extended period of time will cause some of the potassium bitartrate to precipitate. But unless the grapes had an abnormal level of tartrate salts to begin with, it will reduce overall acidity only slightly, perhaps .05%. It helps to add $1/2$ tsp. per gallon of cream of tartar (from the spice rack) as seed crystals when the wine is completely chilled. Once precipitation starts, the process will gain momentum. An old refrigerator or walk–in cooler is an ideal way to keep a steady, controlled temperature for the two to three weeks necessary to completely cold stabilize a wine. Storing the wine outside during late fall and early winter is also satisfactory, although some will go back into suspension if the temperature warms. So rack on the coldest day that comes along.

Cold fermenting

Fermenting over an extended period of time at 45–50° with a cold–tolerant yeast will cause some of the tartrates to settle out for the same reason as cold stabilization — tartrates are less soluble as the temperature falls and alcohol level rises. Rack the wine off the "mud" during a cold spell and the crystals will be left behind.

Carbonic maceration

Carbonic maceration (Chapter 11) is also an effective way to lower total acid. Not all of the malic will disappear, but there will be no lactic acid formed to replace it, as in the case of malolactic fermentation.

Chapter Ten

FERMENTING VARIATIONS – WHITE WINES

he urge to make a better wine runs very high in winemakers! You will soon find yourself contemplating techniques that might be used to improve your work product. Here are some variations in the basic fermentation process which might improve your wine. Although a better wine can never be guaranteed, none of the variations will diminish the quality of your wine (although there is always a risk of spoilage if you are striving for malolactic fermentation).

Soak on the skins

White grapes are often soaked on the skins for a period of time after crushing and sulfiting but before pressing in an attempt to release more of the flavor and varietal characteristic from the skins. Extended soaking for more than a few hours should be done at temperatures below 50°. Without access to a walk–in cooler, the home winemaker should be content with an overnight soaking, or perhaps a day or two with some ice jugs suspended in it.

Soaking on the skins is widely believed to increase the varietal characteristic of the grape in the finished wine. Most of my finest white wines were soaked on the skins before fermentation. On the other hand, I have other pre–soaked wines that picked up an objectionable grassy or herbaceous flavor that I suspect came from the skins. So there is no simple answer as to how much skin contact is optimum.

There are so many variables in making wines that one can never be sure of the reason for differing results. Almost any generalization can be debated. And what is true for one year or one vineyard will not hold true for the next. So the following guidelines should be considered with that in mind.

Firstly, if you suspect that the grapes are still coated with sulfur from late or excessive spraying, don't soak them. Press the clusters whole without even crushing. If they were crushed and soaked, more sulfur would wash off the skins, end up in the must and be converted to H_2S during fermentation. In addition, if you suspect residual sulfur, add $1/2$ tsp. of D.A.P. per 5 gallons to reduce the tendency to generate hydrogen sulfide.

Grapes that are in poor condition should not be soaked on the skins; skin contact should be minimized. In fact, if the grapes have sunburned and broken skins, low acid, bunchrot or some other defect, consider pressing without first crushing in order to minimize skin contact. And give them the maximum of 120 ppm of sulfite. Pressing without crushing will result in a slightly higher acid level, since the free run juice near the outer surface of the grapes is higher in acid.

The high acid level in under–ripe grapes could be reduced slightly by soaking on the skins and pressing twice. The second pressing will extract more of the juice from the center of the grape which will have slightly lower acidity. Soaking on the skins should also bring out more of the varietal characteristic since the flavors in under–ripe grapes will not yet be fully developed.

Grape type is another consideration. Chardonnay is commonly soaked on the skins as the varietal character is inherently so low that it always needs to be enhanced. Sauvignon blanc is often soaked. But gewurztraminer, semillon and the muscat varieties usually are not. On the other hand, I have made some wonderful semillons which were soaked on the skins. The rules in this game are made to be broken!

Note that crushed grapes should be kept as cool as possible while soaking. Keep the container out of direct sunlight. If it is particularly warm at the time, drop in a couple of plastic milk jugs of ice (secure cap) and stir the mass occasionally, which will lower the overall temperature. Extended soaking for 3 or 4 days requires refrigeration. If you are fortunate enough to have access to a walk–in cooler or spare refrigerator, put a layer or two of plastic wrap over the crushed grapes to retain the SO_2 and keep oxygen away and let them soak.

Cold ferment

One can never go wrong by fermenting a white wine slowly over a period of weeks or even months under cool conditions! Slow fermentation at 50° – 55° will preserve more of the bouquet and fruitiness. Steinberg is an excellent yeast for cold fermenting because it slows as the temperature falls but doesn't stop completely until the temperature gets quite low — below 40°. Steinberg was previously used extensively in the commercial fermentation of white wines but has lost ground to the more vigorous and faster Epernay 2, presumably so the wineries don't have to tie up their fermenting capacity as long. Epernay 2 is also used for cold fermenting but stops before Steinberg as the temperature is reduced. It tends to leave a little residual sugar, which is often desired in reislings and gewurtztraminers. Prise de Mousse is also a good yeast for cold fermenting. My preference is Steinberg because it produces a wine with more structure.

Stop fermentation before completion

Rather than letting the wine ferment to dryness and adding sugar back, the better practice is to stop fermentation when unfermented sugar has dropped to the desired level. This is accomplished by fermenting at a cooler temperature and/or using a slower yeast, such as Steinberg or Epernay. It also helps to deprive the yeast of nutrients by racking the juice off the pulp before fermentation and fermenting only the supernatant juice, adding no D.A.P. or yeast food of any type. If these measures are not taken, the wine will quickly ferment right past the desired sugar level before you can intervene.

When Clinitest indicates that unfermented sugar has dropped to its predetermined level, the slowly fermenting wine should be racked, sulfited and chilled. With dry white table wines, the normal dose of $1/4$ tsp. of sulfite per 5 gallons will suffice to prevent renewed fermentation if the wine is kept as cold as possible until it has cleared. However, if you want a sweet wine or if the grapes had significant *botrytis cinerea* (the "noble rot"), the dosage should be increased to $1/2$ tsp. of meta per five gallons and potassium sorbate used as well to inhibit renewed fermentation. Stopping fermentation before total dryness is a natural complement to slow, cold fermentation of wines to be left with significant residual sugar, such as reislings or gewurtztraminers. Without extra meta and sorbate, fermentation could restart. Again, keep it well chilled until it has clarified further and been racked again.

Note that stopping fermentation will keep the alcohol level slightly lower. If your grapes had a high sugar content, such that you are concerned about a "hot" wine (i.e., where the alcohol detracts from aesthetics), stopping fermentation at 1% RS, for example, would keep the alcohol lower by about .55%.

Some winemakers routinely stop fermentation on all their white wines rather than fermenting them dry and adding back sugar. This is the better technique. The only drawback in racking and sulfiting before complete fermentation is that it takes longer to clarify. For some reason, the wine clears more readily if it is allowed to ferment all the way to dryness and the gross lees allowed to settle before being racked. But this is not a major problem as it will usually clear anyway, given more time.

Ferment the free-run must separately

Wineries and home winemakers alike often ferment the free run juice separately. As the crushed grapes are poured into the press basket, about half of the total juice will flow through before pressing even begins. This is known as the "free run" must and will usually have slightly higher sugar and slightly higher acid than the pressed juice. The free–run must is widely believed to produce a higher quality white wine.

Pour the crushed grapes into the press basket and catch the free run juice as it drains. Add the usual $1/4$ tsp. of meta per 5 gallons and transfer it to carboys to let the pulp settle out. If you also wanted to pre–fine with bentonite, this would be the time to do it. (See the next section). Rack the clear juice off the pulp the next morning. This is one situation where the addition of yeast food is indicated if a dry wine is the goal, because the discarded pulp contains a lot of nutrients. Adding D.A.P., yeast extract or a balanced yeast food along with the yeast starter will encourage fermentation to complete dryness.

With 200 pounds of grapes, you will have approximately 6 gallons of free run juice, which will be enough to fill a carboy after fermentation is complete. Ferment 3 gallons in one carboy and 3 gallons in another and combine them near the end of fermentation. Ferment the hard–pressed juice and pulp separately in a third container. If you do not detect enough difference between the free run wine and the pressed, the two can be blended after completion of fermentation. Note, however, that the difference between the two lots might not become apparent for six months or a year, when they are more delicate.

I once fermented 4 gallons of pure pulp from three different varieties of white grapes. The pulp compacted during fermentation and the resulting 3 gallons of wine was initially very clean and delicate, although light bodied. After a year in the bottle, it had lost all its fruit and seemed quite acidic and alcoholic, even though both were lower than the clear juice. This to my mind gives credibility to the practice of commercial wineries of settling and discarding the pulp and fermenting only the clear juice.

Pre-fine with bentonite

Some wineries routinely press without first crushing and centrifuge the must in a nitrogen atmosphere in order to minimize skin and air contact and eliminate unwanted solids before fermentation. This is not an option for the home winemaker. However, you can accomplish somewhat the same result by fining the free–run must with bentonite before fermentation, letting the pulp and bentonite settle overnight and fermenting only the supernatant juice.

Crush, sulfite and press as usual; then stir in the bentonite slurry while transferring to carboys and let it settle overnight. Rack it off the pulp and finings the next morning, add the yeast starter and ferment as you otherwise would. Again, without the nutrients from the pulp, it would be good practice to add a balanced yeast food or D.A.P. if a dry wine is desired.

Ferment the dregs and leftovers

It's fun to ferment the pulp and leftovers from several different varieties together to make what I very loosely label as a "cuvée." Keep adding the lees, sediment, yeast "mud" and excess volumes of the different varieties as you rack and consolidate carboys. Add the mud, even if it's all that remains from a racking! You might end up with 50% solids. It doesn't look very appealing but after a few months on the lees with an occassional stirring, the wine will acquire a delicious, yeasty flavor. Make sure each container is fully topped up when the wine finishes fermenting and add $1/2$ tsp. of meta per 5 gallons. In the interim, keep it cool and stir up the lees occasionally with a heavy dowel. On more than one occasion, my *cuvée* was my best white wine of the year! A venture of this nature obviously assumes you encountered no H_2S during fermentation.

Malolactic fermentation

It is more difficult to induce in white wines, and it diminishes the fruitiness. But MLF adds a unique, "buttery" flavor and is a very good way to lower acidity. See Chapter 12— Malolactic Fermentation.

Chapter Eleven

FERMENTING VARIATIONS – RED WINES

here are fewer fermenting alternatives for red wines than whites. Red wines are typically fermented to complete dryness and bottled with no residual sugar. The principal variable is the length of time the grapes are in contact with the skins and seeds. Malolactic fermentation is covered separately in Chapter 12.

Cold soaking

Red grapes can be soaked on the skins for a few days prior to fermentation. The wineries that do so are of the opinion that cold soaking deepens the color of the wine. It also gives the berries time to disintegrate before fermentation. Crush, de–stem and sulfite as usual; pectic enzyme could also be used to good advantage. Lay some strips of plastic wrap over the surface and chill to 40 – 50° for four or five days. Then add the yeast starter and gradually raise the temperature to 70 – 85°. Access to a walk–in cooler is almost a necessity to cold soak for 4 or 5 days.

Extended maceration

Most red wines are pressed when the unfermented sugar level has dropped to around 0° Brix, by which time it will have picked up maximum color and sufficient tannin and complexity. After all, the more skin contact, the more aging time will be required. Five or six days of fermentation on the skins is sufficient to satisfy most winemakers.

Commercial wineries working with high quality grapes and wanting to extract the maximum flavor often leave the wine on the skins after fermentation ceases. The still wine is held in air–tight vats for a period of time ranging from several days to several weeks. During this period of time the air space in the container is kept flooded with an inert gas to prevent exposure to air. The color will not get deeper during extended maceration; in fact it might get lighter. But extraction of tannin and phenols will increase as they are more soluble in alcohol than water. Interestingly, the added complexity comes from the seeds, not the skins.

There is no consensus as to when pressing should take place, but most commercial winemakers will press after two to three weeks of total time in contact with the skins, including fermentation time. The wine will fall still after 12 to 13 days of fermentation, and be pressed a few days after. The vintner will taste the wine on a daily basis, awaiting a change in the chemical makeup up in the tannin. One day the wine will suddenly taste softer, as though it has aged much longer than it really has. The wine will be pressed within a day or two. If pressing is delayed, it will become more tannic. So pressing takes place during this short window of opportunity.

Here's how you can do extended maceration with an ordinary primary fermenter and lid. Crush, ferment and punch down as usual for red grapes. Once the sugar level has dropped to 0° B. on the saccharometer, start laying strips of plastic wrap over the now diminished cap. The plastic wrap will trap the slight amount of CO_2 still being produced, hold it next to the wine and keep air away. Continue punching down, but once a day will suffice. Replace the plastic wrap and fermenter lid each time. The wine should be tasted every day from now on. It will still taste harsh and bitter, but it will mellow dramatically one day soon.

After 12 or 13 days with the ambient temperature held at approximately 75°, fermentation will be complete. This should be confirmed with Clinitest, not a saccharometer. Malolactic fermentation might also be complete, particularly if you inoculated right after fermentation started. Run a chromatography test now if you are curious. *Appendix A.* If it is complete, you will want to sulfite and chill the wine at the time of pressing.

There is no hard-and-fast rule as to how long the wine should be left in contact with the skins and seeds. Some home winemakers (and wineries as well) like to wait until the cap has sunk before pressing. This will occur when MLF is complete and when most of the trapped carbon dioxide has escaped. However, by waiting until the cap sinks, you might miss the window of opportunity, when the tannin has softened. The better practice is to press by taste.

In most cases the softening will be so dramatic as to leave no doubt. A wine that one day is totally undrinkable will the next day be excitingly mellow; the fruit and flavor will be overwhelming. This is the time to press. Pressing could wait a few more days without permanently damaging the wine; but the longer you wait, the longer it will take to age. What you want to avoid is leaving it on the skins for two or three weeks after the softening. If you miss a day or two of sample tasting and think the window might have slipped by, my suggestion is to press no later than three weeks after crushing, just to avoid the possibility of undue harshness. Note that although the softening will normally occur between two and three weeks, it is somewhat temperature dependent and could take longer if the ambient temperature was less than 75°.

Using this technique and always keeping the remains of the cap covered with plastic wrap, you can safely extend the maceration for several days beyond the end of fermentation without ruining the wine.

Make a rosé

Good rosés are not appreciated in the United States to the extent that a winery can afford to divert quality red grapes, such as cabernet sauvignon, merlot or zinfandel. This is not a consideration for the home winemaker because the cost is the same either way. In fact, by drawing off part of a red grape must that has fermented on the skins for only a short while, you might end up with the best of both worlds — a delicious rosé and a highly–extracted red wine of better quality than it otherwise would be.

Crush and de–stem the grapes as though a red table wine were to be made, using $1/4$ tsp. of meta to discourage malolactic fermentation, which is not desirable in rosés. Prepare a yeast starter solution and inoculate the must as usual. After it has fermented on the skins for a few hours or perhaps a day or two, dip out part of the must and transfer it to a carboy to ferment to dryness.

The question of when the rosé portion should be drawn off is a decision that is largely personal to your goal. The longer it is left to ferment on the skins, of course, the more color and complexity it will acquire. And the longer it will take to mature. Check the color frequently, and when it looks right to you, make the transfer. Let it get a little darker than you think you would like because the color will lighten as the solids precipitate and the wine clears.

Continue fermenting the rosé portion separately, in a carboy, as though it were a white wine. The procedure for fermenting and clarifying white wines should be followed from this point forward. After the wine is still and the gross lees have settled, add some cane or beet sugar back to raise residual sugar to the desired level. You could stop fermentation at the desired point by racking, sulfiting and chilling. Since most people expect a touch of sweetness in a rosé, residual sugar should probably be at least 1% and perhaps as high as 3%.

Meanwhile, continue fermenting the rest of the original must as you would a normal red table wine. Punch the cap down twice daily and press when the unfermented sugar reaches 0° Brix. Since all of the skins are concentrated in a smaller volume of wine, the extraction of phenols and intensity of flavors should be higher. If you want malolactic fermentation in this portion, add the starter right after the rosé portion is removed.

The entire crushing could be fermented into a rosé. Crush–destem, sulfite and ferment the entire crushing on the skins for a day or two until the desired color is attained. Then press and finish in carboys as you would a white wine.

In years when red grapes don't ripen and will not make a premium dry red table wine due to high acidity, it will be easier to get desirable red *vinifera* grapes such as cabernet sauvignon. The higher acidity can be countered with higher residual sugar.

Carbonic maceration

Carbonic maceration is a good way to lower total acidity and end up with a unique red wine in the process. The grapes are not even crushed; they are placed in an air–free atmosphere and "cooked" at 80° to 90° for two or three weeks. It is the natural enzymes within the berry, not yeast, that convert the sugar to alcohol. The resulting wine is relatively low in tannin, very dark in color and has an unusual fruity quality that you will either like or dislike.

Carbonic maceration is often used to enhance wine made from under-ripe, high-acid grapes of lesser quality. It can be used with premium fruit as well but seems to capture less of the fruit flavor than conventional fermentation. Regardless of the fruit, the challenge is keeping air out until the enzyme process starts and begins generating its own CO_2, as the grapes would spoil quickly if exposed to air at the higher temperatures necessary to initiate the enzyme process.

The ideal procedure would consist of completely filling an air–tight container with whole clusters of red grapes, displacing the air with CO_2, sealing it against air penetration and returning to press after about three weeks at 85°. A stainless steel vat with floating lid would be an ideal piece of equipment for carbonic maceration, as would a Graf poly container, since both are air tight and have an air lock. But let's assume you have nothing to ferment it in other than a Rubbermaid Brute® primary fermenter and lid and want to try carbonic maceration. Here's one way it can be done.

As soon as the grapes arrive, crush and de–stem about 10% of the batch. Initiate fermentation in this portion with a dependable wine yeast, such as Prise de Mousse, before adding the grape clusters. The purpose of fermenting this small batch of ordinary red grape must is to generate sufficient CO_2 to displace the air in the container and protect the grapes until the enzyme process starts a few days later.

Once fermentation has started in this small batch, dump it into the container. Now add the remaining 90%, which will be whole clusters on the stems. Ideally, the container would be full to the top. Put the lid in place and tape it with many layers of duct tape. You probably will not be able to totally seal the container, so tape it as best you can.

To be on the safe side, I would also recommend drilling a $3/8$ inch hole in the lid and inserting a straight–stem air lock so that CO_2 gas can be transferred from a carboy of fermenting wine or sugar water. See *Appendix C*. Since you will not know for sure how fast the sugar is being converted to alcohol or when it slows down or stops, plan to press two to three weeks after the container is sealed. If you cannot keep the room temperature at 85°, wrap the container with an electric blanket set on high.

When the container is opened in two or three weeks, the grapes will look almost the same as the day they were added. But they will have lost all their structure and firmness and will collapse with the slightest pressure. There will be a considerable amount of wine accumulated at the bottom of the container, consisting of the original fermented portion plus additional juice that dripped out of the clusters during maceration. This can be racked out before pressing and kept separate as it has less carbonic flavor than the wine remaining in the clusters.

Both portions will still have several points of unfermented sugar and should be fermented to dryness under air lock. The two lots can be combined at pressing. Or they can be fermented to dryness separately and blended later, or not, as appeals to you. The pressed portion will have more carbonic flavor than the other.

Here is a variation that can be used to add a touch of the carbonic flavor to a traditional fermentation. Set aside a small part of the grape clusters before crushing and de–stemming, at most 10%. After the main portion has been crushed and de–stemmed, add the whole clusters back and ferment normally in an open primary fermenter but at 80 – 85°, punch down, etc. The carbonic process will take place within the whole berries and become part of the overall wine when everything is pressed. But the carbonic quality will be less pronounced.

Pinot noir and gamay grapes are the classic grapes for carbonic maceration. In my opinion the flavor of these grape types is highly compatible with the carbonic flavor that results. Since these two varieties are low in tannin, it is better to use whole clusters; the resulting wine will still be low in tannin. If you are using red grapes which have more tannin, such as cabernet sauvignon or zinfandel, the grapes could be stripped off the stems to keep the tannin level lower. But even with cabernet sauvignon, I have found the tannin level to be high but not ruinously so as a result of using whole clusters.

Chapter Twelve

MALOLACTIC FERMENTATION

alolactic fermentation (MLF) imparts a unique flavor which is particularly noticeable in white wines, takes some of the sharpness off the acid as it is perceived around the edge of the tongue and "rounds out" a wine. MLF is most commonly sought in dry red table wines, provided must acidity is not too low to start with. It is also used for some dry white wines, such as chardonnay, sauvignon blanc and sometimes semillon, but is generally avoided for fruity white wines, such as reisling, gewurztraminer, muscats and chenin blanc. The diacetyl produced by malolactic bacteria is the principal source of the "buttery" quality in chardonnays.

Malolactic bacteria break down the malic acid into lactic acid, producing water and carbon dioxide in the process. Since lactic acid is only half as acidic as malic acid, total acidity is lowered by half the amount of malic acid converted. For example, if the original malic acid content happened to be .4% and all were converted to lactic, total acidity would drop by .2%. MLF is the only practical way for the home winemaker to selectively reduce malic acid without first neutralizing all of the tartaric acid, which is the desirable acid.

Malolactic bacteria occur naturally in the air and on the grapes. If potassium metabisulfite is omitted, the malolactic bacteria might multiply to the point where they will do their job. But it might not happen until the following spring or summer, if at all. And the wrong strain might develop. Since two of the three strains of malolactic bacteria are undesirable, the better practice is to kill all malolactic bacteria by sulfiting at crushing and inoculating later with a pure strain of the desired bacteria, *leuconostoc oenos*. The outcome is both faster and more certain this way.

Note that potassium sorbate should not be used if you seek malolactic fermentation because it is a nutrient to the bacteria which results in an objectionable "geranium" flavor.

Adverse conditions

Malolactic bacteria are finicky critters. They thrive only under certain conditions and even then, nothing is guaranteed. Here are the conditions in which they struggle. If you want MLF, do your best to *avoid* these conditions:

HIGH ALCOHOL. Malolactic bacteria are not very tolerant of high alcohol levels, which is why it is more difficult to initiate MLF in still wines. If your grapes have high sugar and you want malolactic fermentation, inoculate early in fermentation, before much sugar has been converted to alcohol.

HIGH SULFITE. Malolactic bacteria are much more sensitive to sulfite than yeast. Even a modest level of 25 ppm of free sulfite is likely to kill malolactic bacteria. It is best in my opinion to use $1/4$ tsp. per 5 gallons (= 50 ppm) at the time of the crush. This kills all natural malolactic bacteria, including the bad strains. If you want MLF, inoculate later with a cultured strain.

LOW TEMPERATURES. Most strains of *leuconostoc oenos* are barely active at 65°. The "OSU" strain will work at lower temperatures, but all strains are more active in the desired temperature range of 75 – 80°.

LOW pH. If your grapes have high acid, the pH might be too low to cultivate malolactic bacteria. The traditional malolactic bacteria will work in red wines having a pH of 3.3 or higher and in white wines having a pH of 3.1 or higher. If you do not know the pH of the must but know that total acid is high and want malolactic fermentation to reduce acidity, use calcium carbonate to lower the total acidity to 1.0% before adding the malolactic starter.

Malolactic bacteria might tolerate one adverse condition but not two or three. It is quite easy to avoid MLF — just use sulfite, keep the temperature down and clarify the wine before allowing the temperature to rise, and it would be most unusual to experience any MLF.

It's much more complicated if you want MLF. Great care must be taken to make the conditions as ideal as possible before adding the starter — no free SO_2, temperature at 75 –80° and proper acidity and pH. It also helps to use yeast extract as a nutrient at the rate of ½ g. per gallon and to stir up the lees and nutrients with a slender dowel once or twice a week. Note that although yeast love diammonium phosphate, malolactic bacteria are indifferent to it.

When to inoculate

There is no consensus as to the optimum time to inoculate. It is a fact, however, that it is more difficult to get MLF started after fermentation is over, due to high alcohol, reduced nutrients and absence of heat from fermentation. And it is a fact that the malolactic bacteria very much like the presence of skins. So in the case of red wines, I always add the malolactic starter and yeast extract as soon as fermentation reaches its peak, which is usually two days after the yeast starter was added. If the ML starter is added right after the onset of fermentation and the wine temperature maintained at 80-90°, MLF is often complete by the time you want to press in approximately two weeks.

Malolactic fermentation is not as easily induced in white wines since they are fermented cooler than reds, have fewer nutrients and are not fermented on the skins. It is particularly important to use yeast extract for MLF in white wines. In the case of chardonnay, which is commonly fermented at 65°, you could add the malolactic starter and yeast extract shortly after fermentation becomes vigorous and hope to get it started during primary fermentation. My preference is to wait until the wine is dry and inoculate then. If you wait, I would suggest using a freeze dried strain, such as *Viniflora oenos*, because it is more dependable in still wines. By waiting you will end up with more diacetyl, the source of the buttery quality, because there will be no yeast activity to neutralize it. The tradeoff in waiting is that it is more difficult to initiate MLF in still wines;

and the longer you wait, the more uncertain the proposition becomes.

Note that malolactic fermentation will be easiest to initiate in the carboy having the most pulp and solids. Rather than making a starter, I often concentrate the pulp in one carboy and inoculate that carboy with the starter. Once MLF is established, a pint or quart of the pulp can be transferred to the other carboys. One package of starter can be made to work for much more than 5 gallons this way.

When is MLF complete?

It is important to know when MLF is complete because the temperature should be lowered as soon afterward as possible. The higher temperatures and lack of meta needed to support MLF create a high risk of undesirable side reactions. This risk is drastically reduced when the temperature is lowered and meta added. You also want to know whether or not the conversion is complete before bottling as renewed malolactic activity in the bottle could ruin the wine.

There are several ways to determine when all the malic acid has been converted to lactic, the simplest being to watch the bubble activity closely. MLF generates tiny bubbles of CO_2. Give the carboy a quick twist and a rush of small bubbles is a good indication of malolactic activity, particularly if Clinitest indicates that the wine is bone dry. If the conditions were right, and it appeared that MLF started, and the temperature has been constantly maintained at 65° or more, the conversion will probably be complete when the bubbles slow noticeably or stop. This is an acceptable method of monitoring MLF, although not the most reliable.

You could supplement bubble watching with periodic titration tests, which will indicate reductions in total acidity. When total acid stops falling and the bubbles slow or stop, MLF is presumably complete, again assuming proper conditions and a temperature continuously above 65°.

Paper chromatography is the best way of testing for completion of MLF. A test kit is not prohibitively expensive or difficult to use. *Appendix A.* With red wines, a test should be run as soon as it is dry. Occasionally, MLF will be complete by then, in which case the wine should immediately be racked, sulfited and chilled to reduce the risk of spoilage. If MLF is not complete, hold the temperature at 70 – 75° until it finishes, which will usually be another month or two.

Once you have malolactic fermentation underway, do your utmost to get it go to completion without interruption. Keep the temperature up and stir up the lees twice weekly with a slender dowel. It is not only a matter of wanting to finish MLF so that the wine can be cold stabilized during the depth of winter — you want to avoid the risk of renewed MLF after bottling. If you let the temperature fall, for instance, malolactic fermentation would stop, but the bacteria will not necessarily die. Activity might or might not resume the following summer. If it does not, you might be forced to bottle with incomplete MLF, only to have it resume after bottling, even if you sulfited before bottling. With no way for the bacterial odor and gases to escape the bottle, the wine would probably be ruined. That's why it is good practice to run a chromatography test before bottling.

If a wine has gone through MLF and the acid drops so low that it has to be increased, be sure to use tartaric acid rather than malic. Malic acid would be an invitation to renewed activity.

Stuck MLF

If malolactic fermentation appears to have stopped but a chromatography test reveals the process to be only partially complete, it has stuck. This usually occurs when the wine was too cold for too long — it can be difficult to get it going again. Raise the temperature to 70 –75° and add a teaspoon of yeast extract. Stir up the lees with your dowel two or three times a week, and it will probably start again. If it does not, add a fresh starter. Again, *Viniflora oenos*, is more dependable in still wines.

Precautions

The absence of meta in combination with higher temperatures creates a situation that is ripe for spoilage problems. The wine should not be exposed to any air in this vulnerable state. The bit of CO_2 generated by MLF will protect it from air and acetobacter. Acetobacter, which cannot form without oxygen, is indicated by a white film or crust on the surface in the neck of the carboy. It is a precursor to vinegar and even trace amounts are objectionable. If a white crust does appear in the neck of the carboy, the best remedy is to insert a small tube into the wine, add a bit of water or sound wine and float the scum out of the carboy, as it is almost impossible to spoon or siphon it out. A tiny burette funnel and small tube make this procedure easier. Then rack, sulfite ($1/4$ tsp./ 5 gal.) and cool. If a surface film does develop, just hope the wine is not already ruined. A heavy dose of meta might help deal with the off–flavor but there is no actual cure.

The risk of acetobacter can be reduced by occasionally adding a tablespoon of brandy in the neck of the carboy. Better yet, spray a mist of Everclear over the surface, as wineries do. The alcohol kills the bacteria.

If you have tried everything and cannot get MLF to go to completion, go ahead and bottle anyway. The wine itself will not be inferior if only part of the malic acid is converted. The risk of post–bottling MLF can be reduced if 75 ppm of meta is used at bottling. This is a fairly heavy dose which will give the bouquet a sulfite bite for a while, but it will disappear in a few months. The risk of post–bottling MLF can be further reduced if you have the means to super–chill the wine down to 25° for a week or two, which tends to kill the bacteria.

If this is your first effort at home winemaking, I suggest that you wait a season or two before attempting malolactic fermentation. The limited use of sulfite and higher temperatures required to induce MLF greatly increase the risk of ruining your wine. In addition to increasing the spoilage risk, malolactic fermentation reduces the fruity quality in the wine which in my opinion is a negative.

Malolactic Bacteria Glossary

Several different strains of cultured malolactic bacteria have been isolated and developed commercially. Most wine supply stores will carry one or two different strains. Some strains produce much more diacetyl than others. Some work at lower pH than others, and some at lower temperatures. Here are some notes on those that are often available.

VINIFLORA OENOS by Chr. Hansen (Denmark). This is a very good product and is the best choice to inoculate a still wine. It can be added directly to the wine without the nuisance of having to make a starter solution several days before inoculating. It is freeze–dried and will keep a season or two in the freezer, as long as the foil packet has not been opened. Once opened, it has to be used immediately as it is very sensitive to humidity. This is a good choice to induce MLF in a still chardonnay. Add it after the wine is still to maximize the buttery quality. If added before fermentation is complete, the yeast will neutralize some of the diacetyl, the source of the buttery flavor.

OREGON STATE UNIVERSITY STRAIN. This strain was isolated for use on the low pH pinot noirs from Oregon's Willamette Valley. I like it not so much because it is said to work as low as 2.9 pH, but because it is more active in the 65 – 70° range. It is easier to maintain this temperature during winter months than 75–80°, as required by the other strains. This strain is marketed by Lallemand as "OSU" and by Wyeast Laboratories, Mt. Hood, Oregon, as "Vintner's Choice." The latter is in liquid form in foil packets which can be added directly without making a starter solution.

LALLEMAND X–3. This is a good combination of four different strains. It comes in dried form (not freeze-dried), but making a starter solution is easy. Lallemand markets several other strains as well.

TWO–PART STARTERS. The traditional two–part, wet malolactic starter is the least expensive but must be activated a week before inoculating and given time to completely convert all malic acid in the starter sample to lactic acid. Ideally, this would be confirmed by chromatography before inoculating because MLF is not likely to start unless the conversion is complete.

Chapter Thirteen

SPARKLING WINES

 parkling wines from the Champagne area of France are the only ones which can rightfully be called "champagne." However, fine sparkling wines come from many other parts of the world; and there is no reason your cellar could not be added to the list! The home winemaker can in fact make first class sparkling wines — far better than you ever expect. But you have to start with good fruit, and it takes patience. The technique described below — known to the French as *méthode champenoise* — is the best process there is for making sparkling wines, whether it be with pinot noir, chardonnay, riesling, peaches or apricots. The discussion that follows is in terms of white grape juice but the same technique would work for peaches or apricots as long as the acid level is raised to .7% or more.

Méthode champenoise

The goal initially is to make a sound dry white table wine having alcohol in the range of 10 to 11%. The first fermentation is known as the *cuvée* fermentation and is done by home winemakers in carboys in essentially the same manner as set forth in Chapter 2 for regular white table wines. Except that the grapes are picked when the sugar level is 18–20° Brix. After the *cuvée* has been fermented, racked and clarified, a measured amount of sugar and fresh yeast starter are added and the wine is bottled and capped.

The sugar ferments slowly in the bottle; it is this *tirage* fermentation which gives the wine its effervescence.

After the *tirage* fermentation, the wine is aged on the lees in the bottle for a period of time ranging from several months to several years. Then the bottles are "riddled." Riddling, or *remuage* to the French, is the process of manipulating the lees into the neck of the bottle with sharp twists of the bottle. The bottles are held at an angle in a rack and the angle is gradually increased until the rack is flat and the bottles vertical.

Next, a small plug of ice is frozen in the neck of the bottle to hold the lees in place. When the bottle is tipped to a 45° angle and the cap removed, the lees are blown out along with the ice plug. The wine is now "disgorged." A measured amount of sugar syrup — the *dosage* — is quickly added to sweeten the remaining wine. The bottle is then permanently closed. This is the essence of *méthode champenoise*, used by makers of fine sparkling wines throughout the world.

Grapes for sparkling wines

Although pinot noir and chardonnay are the classic grape types for French champagnes, other varieties also work well, including semillon, sauvignon blanc and reisling or blends thereof. Grapes for sparkling wines are picked at an earlier stage of ripeness — typically between 18 and 20° Brix — in order to produce a still wine with only 10% – 11% alcohol before bottle fermentation. A lower level of alcohol is desired because sugar will be added for bottle fermentation and that will raise the alcohol level to the desired level of 13% or so. If you started with grapes having a Brix of 24°, the wine would have 13% alcohol after the *cuvée* fermentation. It would be difficult to initiate bottle fermentation with 13% alcohol; and even if successful, the finished wine would have alcohol of 14 1/2% after bottle fermentation. That is too high. So it works best to use grapes having a Brix of 18 to 20°.

Ideally, total acid of the grapes would be .75 –.80%. But the acid usually will not have dropped to that level when the sugar is still below 20° B. So acid of 1% or more is to be expected when grapes are picked at 18 – 20° Brix. Higher acid can be countered with a higher level of residual sugar when the dosage is added.

Crushing and pressing

White grapes, such as chardonnay, are crushed, pressed and processed as though you were setting out to make a typical dry white table wine, as described in Chapter 2. However, if you are processing red grapes, such as pinot noir, you will need to decide before crushing whether you want a sparkling white wine or a blush or a rosé. Although pinot noir grapes are red, the juice is white. But if crushed and left on the skins, the wine will absorb pigment from the skins. The higher the alcohol level, the faster the juice will become colored. Coloration can be completely avoided if the grapes are pressed without first being crushed. The resulting white wine is known and marketed as *"blanc de noirs"* to distinguish it from a *"blanc de blancs"* made from white grapes.

On the other hand, if you want enough color that a blush wine will result, the grapes should be crushed and soaked on the skins for a while and then pressed and fermented. If you want an even darker, rosé–type sparkling wine, crush, de–stem and ferment on the skins for a short while before pressing. The higher the alcohol, the more quickly the color is leached out of the skins.

Many champagne producers press only lightly for their premium bottlings without crushing first. The lightly–pressed pomace is then crushed and pressed again to make a sparkling wine of somewhat lesser quality. Blending of varieties and vintages is also common, particularly in the Champagne region of France, where some varieties do not ripen sufficiently every year.

Whether processing red grapes or white grapes, meta should be carefully limited to $1/4$ tsp. per 5 gallons at pressing. This will be sufficient to discourage malolactic fermentation which is not desired in sparkling wines. Since grapes of this type are typically low in tannin, I like to add $1/4 - 1/2$ tsp. of tannin per 5 gallons at pressing as an aid in clarifying.

Although almost any strain of yeast could be used for the *cuvée* fermentation, I am partial to cold fermenting with Steinberg yeast when working with pinot noir or chardonnay to preserve as much of the fruit and bouquet as possible.

Cuvée fermentation

The *cuvée* fermentation takes place in carboys filled to about ¾ capacity and topped with air locks. When unfermented sugar is nearing 0° B., the carboys are combined or topped up and the temperature raised to about 70° to encourage complete fermentation. When Clinitest confirms that it is dry, the carboys should be topped up again if necessary and the wine cold stabilized for one to two months.

Racking, fining and clarifying

The challenge of clarifying is the same as it is with any white wine. Follow the procedures in Chapter 2, with one exception. Since you want no free SO_2 in solution when the *tirage* yeast is added for bottle fermentation, meta should be omitted entirely at the last racking. This is when the wine is re–inoculated with a fresh yeast starter, bottled and *tirage* fermentation initiated. Everything else is the same.

You would like the wine to be crystal clear before the sugar is added for bottle fermentation because if it isn't clear by then, you'll never be able to clear it in the bottle. If the second fining attempt is not a total success and the wine has been cold stabilized for several months, proceed with bottle fermentation anyway. The haze will be an aesthetic negative but will not diminish the flavor.

Choice of bottles

Whether you plan to purchase new bottles or soak labels off used bottles and clean them up, they should be heavy sparkling wine bottles of U.S. origin free of chips or flaws. Avoid sparkling cider bottles and any that are not heavy enough to withstand the high pressure that will build up after bottle fermentation. Bottles made in the U.S. are preferable because the neck is the right diameter to accommodate a standard crown cap such as is used for beer or soda pop. Rather than inserting a mushroom cork or plastic cap, U.S. sparkling wine producers simply cap the bottles with a crown cap for the *tirage* fermentation. You want to be able to do the same, since a crown cap is much easier to put on and take off. Bottles from Spain, France and Italy have a larger neck diameter which a crown cap will not fit.

Bottles having any stain or mold in them should also be discarded — they're not worth the effort. It is important that bottles for sparkling wines be carefully cleaned with a brush to remove any stain or invisible film they may contain. The cleaner the glass, the more freely the sediment will slip down into the neck of the bottle when it is riddled.

Bottling and *tirage* fermentation

After several months of cold stabilization and two or perhaps three rackings, the *cuvée* wine will be totally dry and hopefully crystal clear. It will be either white or blush as planned and will have alcohol in the 10 to 11% range. Total acid will have dropped slightly from its pre–fermentation level. Other types of wine might have been blended along the way if you had them on hand and felt experimental.

The procedure for making sparkling wines now departs from that for dry white table wines: it is time to add a measured amount of sugar, inoculate with a fresh yeast starter and bottle the wine for the *tirage* fermentation. The more sugar you add, the more carbonated the wine will be. Add too much, and you'll have bottles exploding all over the place! So the amount of sugar has to be carefully measured to stay within the limits of the bottle strength.

Although champagne bottles will withstand pressures of 8 or 10 atmospheres, commercial winemakers seldom exceed 6 atmospheres of bottle pressure. It is better for the home winemaker to limit it to 4 atmospheres. This will provide an abundance of carbonation without running the risk of exploding bottles. In fact, there would be nothing wrong with adding only enough sugar to produce two atmospheres of pressure and ending up with a creamy, spritzy wine known in France as a *crémant*. The amount of carbonation and the alcohol level are far less important in the case of sparkling wines than is the quality of the grapes and the time spent on the lees.

Four grams of sugar per liter will generate one atmosphere of pressure after bottle fermentation. To produce four atmospheres, therefore, you will need 16 grams of sugar per liter. This is the equivalent of 2¹/₈ ounces per gallon. But before doing the calculations, do another Clinitest just to make sure there is no unfermented sugar left in the wine. If there is, convert the percentage to grams or ounces and deduct it from your calculations.

It will be more difficult to initiate the *tirage* fermentation than the initial fermentation. In addition to 10 or 11% alcohol, the wine has been clarified and has a low nutrient level compared to the original must. This combination of factors creates a rather hostile atmosphere in which to re–initiate fermentation. So it has to be done with some care. Here is how to handle this critical stage.

Choice of yeast is important for bottle fermentation. You want a yeast which is vigorous and alcohol–tolerant, making Prise de Mousse a good choice. Surprisingly, Pasteur Champagne is not recommended. California Champagne yeast (UCD #505) would be an excellent choice since it coagulates and clears so readily; but it is difficult to locate. So you will probably find yourself using Prise de Mousse.

Before activating the yeast, a sugar syrup should be made by dissolving a carefully calculated and weighed amount of cane or beet sugar ($10^1/_2$ ounces per 5 gallons of wine) in an equal volume of warm water or wine. Heat it gently in the microwave if necessary to dissolve it. Set the syrup aside to cool.

Now activate two packets of the dry yeast in four ounces of warm water as explained in Chapter 2. After the yeast is re–hydrated, rack the *cuvée* into a large pail or primary fermenter and add the sugar syrup and activated yeast plus $1/_2$ tsp. of diammonium phosphate per 5 gallons. Also add about 2 ounces of liquid beermaker's isinglass. The isinglass will help clarification after bottle fermentation by coagulating with the yeast hulls. You can also add another $1/_4$ to $1/_2$ tsp. of tannin at this time, dissolved in water, because most of the tannin that was previously added will have precipitated with the first dose of isinglass. And some of the tannin being added now will precipitate with the additional isinglass being added. Any excess will oxidize during the years it spends on the lees.

After everything is mixed up in the pail and stirred a bit for aeration, the wine should be immediately racked into the champagne bottles, which should previously have been thoroughly washed, brushed and rinsed. Use your dowel to stir up the yeast in the pail occasionally while racking — solids tend to settle rather quickly and you want some yeast in each bottle.

Leave about an inch of air space in each bottle. Use a bottle capper to seal the bottles with crown caps, and mark the side of each bottle with a piece of masking tape or paint stripe. This reference point is needed so the bottles can be returned to the same position each time after being shaken during the months to come.

The bottles should be stored at 55° to 60°, not over 65°, for two or three months while bottle fermentation takes place. Shake each bottle once a week for the first month to disperse the yeast and return it to the same position, tape marker up. It is always advisable to wear protective goggles and gloves while shaking bottles in case one of the bottles is cracked or has a flaw. After three months, bottle fermentation should be complete, but the time can vary.

The natural desire is to get on with the process so you can start drinking your wine! But you will be well rewarded by waiting. A goodly portion of the high price tag on vintage champagnes from France is attributable to the time spent on the lees, which could be up to six or seven years. During this period of time the yeast cells die and decompose, which imparts a pleasing flavor. A distinct change in character is said to occur after two years on the lees and another after four or five years. In any event the wine should spend at least one year on the lees before being riddled and disgorged, simply to allow ample time for all the yeast cells to die and settle out. The bottles should be shaken two or three times a year during this time and replaced in the same position, marker up.

Riddling

Aside from a bottle capper, the only additional equipment needed for making sparkling wines is a riddling rack. See *Illustration E*, page 110, for hole diameters and spacing using a standard two–by–two and $1/_2$" plywood for the frame. The type of rack or method of construction is not important, but it should be designed with a pivot point so that the angle can be changed as riddling progresses. A small rack sufficient for 12 bottles should suffice. I built a huge one capable of holding 48 bottles and later discovered that I riddle and disgorge only a case at a time. The longer it takes to get around to building your rack, the more time the wine will have on the lees; so there's no great rush on this project!

When riddling is started, the bottles will be almost horizontal.

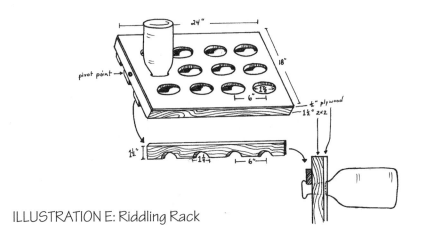

ILLUSTRATION E: Riddling Rack

By the end of riddling, the board will be horizontal and the bottles standing vertically, neck down, with the lees accumulated on the crown cap. Start the riddling process by vigorously shaking each bottle to loosen the lees and stain that accumulated during aging. Because the bottles were faithfully replaced with the tape marker up, the sediment will be limited to one location. Place the bottles, stain now dissolved, in the rack, with the rack positioned so that the bottles rest at about 30° above horizontal. Use the tape marker to place them all in the same relative position.

After a few days the lees will have settled again — it's time for the first riddling installment. Give each bottle a sharp twist 90° in one direction, immediately followed by a sharp twist 45° back toward the original position. Drop it back in the slot with a small jolt which will help break the lees loose from the glass.

This process should be repeated every two or three days until the tape marker indicates that the bottles have been rotated a full 360°. Then change the angle of the rack so that the bottles are closer to upright. Increase the bottle angle to perhaps 45° and repeat the process until they have been rotated another full 360°. Then increase the bottle angle another notch. As the angle gets steeper, the lees will slide toward the neck more willingly and you can rotate them more than +90°/−45° each time. There will ultimately be about one teaspoon of yeast lees and isinglass resting in the neck of each bottle. Once riddled, the bottles can be stored indefinitely, neck down, or you can proceed at once with disgorging.

Disgorging, adding the *dosage* and recapping

The object in disgorging is to freeze an ice plug in the neck of the bottle, pop the cap to blow it out, add a measured quantity of sugar syrup to sweeten the wine and re–cap the bottle. The method I ultimately settled upon for freezing the ice plug is a plywood rack in the freezer. A piece of $1/2$ inch plywood with holes (about $1^3/_8 - 1^1/_2"$ diameter) drilled on six inch centers works well; you might even be able to use the board from your riddling rack. Devise legs as needed to prop up the board in the freezer after it has been loaded with several bottles of wine.

If the freezer is full, chill the wine in a refrigerator for a day. Then get a hefty supply of crushed ice and sprinkle a generous quantity of calcium chloride on the ice to lower the freezing point and stick the necks of the bottles in. I have not tried this, but it would probably work if done on a cold winter day.

I suggest freezing only one bottle initially. Some of this bottle will be used to make the sugar syrup, or *dosage*, and the rest to top up the remaining bottles after the *dosage* is added. Check regularly to determine approximately how long it will take for an ice plug $1^1/_2$ to 2 inches long to form. If the ice plug is much longer, you will lose too much wine when the capped is popped off.

After the ice plug has formed, cradle the bottle in the crook of your arm at a 45° angle and pop the cap off. The ice plug encapsuling the lees will disappear instantly, taking the lees with it, and you will end up with almost 750 ml of clear sparkling wine which is bone dry. Cap this first bottle with a stopper to retain the sparkle and store it in the refrigerator.

While the other 11 bottles are in the freezer, make the *dosage*. How much sugar to add? This takes us back to the topic of residual sugar/total acid discussed in Chapter 3! It's matter of acid level and preference. A "brut" champagne of French origin might have residual sugar of up to 1.5%, a "sec" up to 2.5% and a "demi–sec" up to 4 or 5%. So it depends on your palate.

Assuming that a Clinitest confirms the wine to be totally dry, that you want residual sugar of 1% and that you will be disgorging 11 bottles, you will need to add about 3 ounces of sugar per 11 bottles. (750 ml X 11 X .01 = 82.5 g. = 2.9 ounces). Weigh out the needed amount of sugar and add it to a slightly smaller volume of wine from the first bottle. Better yet, use a good quality brandy. My container of choice is a measuring cup or beaker marked in milliliters. Now gently warm the sugar solution in the microwave as necessary to dissolve the sugar, stir, warm again, stir.

Until now, the yeast lees have been protecting the wine against oxidation. Once the lees are removed, the wine will need some protection in the form of SO_2. When the sugar has dissolved and the syrup cooled, dissolve $1/8$ tsp. of potassium metabisulfite in 11 ml of water. One ml per bottle will raise the level of free SO_2 to about 50 parts per million. This is a bit on the high side and might be detectable right after adding the *dosage* and recorking, particularly since the effervescence will lift it right into your nostrils. However, the free SO_2 will quickly bond to the sugar and will not be noticeable after a few months. It is needed to give your sparkling wine some much needed protection against oxidation. If no sulfite is added at this stage, maderization will probably be noticeable in less than a year.

Divide the total volume of sugar syrup in the beaker or measuring cup by 11 to determine the amount of syrup to be added to each bottle. I use a 10 ml oral dispenser from the drug store to draw out the correct volume of syrup and dispense it into each bottle after it has been opened and disgorged. Also add 1 ml of the sulfide solution with a pipet. Now the bottle should be topped up with dry sparkling wine from the first bottle and quickly corked or capped. Keep the first bottle capped and chilled when not in use to minimize loss of carbonation.

Corking

The classic mushroom–shaped cork is the best closure device but requires a special corker which is a relatively big expense for the limited use it will probably receive. Most home winemakers will be content to use a plastic closure, which can be driven in with a rubber mallet and held in place with a wire basket. Or you could use another crown cap — not very classy but it will do a good job of retaining pressure and keeping air out. Crimp a foil capsule over the neck and the work is done. At last!

As you know by now, *méthode champenoise* is time consuming and labor intensive. If you are willing to make the commitment, consider doubling or tripling the quantity of grapes you normally process. Particularly if high quality fruit at 18° to 19° Brix is available to you. That way, you can enjoy some of the wine while the rest continues to age on the lees. Larger quantities will also allow you to lightly press some of the grapes without crushing and to make a second wine from heavily pressed grapes. And if you decide that the sugar level in the first batch to be disgorged and sweetened is either too high or too low, it can be corrected for the next batch. The key to premium champagne, once again, is starting with premium fruit and aging on the lees.

Chapter Fourteen

ALL ABOUT OAK

any people like an oak flavor in wine, as it adds a distinctive flavor. Although oak barrels are not very practical for the home winemaker, the flavor can be successfully imparted using oak chips, granular oak or oak staves.

Oak should always be used sparingly. A few months after the oak chips have been removed, the oak flavor will have greatly diminished. It might seem like the wine could handle another dose of chips. But don't be tempted! At some unknown point, adding even a small amount of oak produces an overwhelming oak flavor and astringency.

Oak chips, shavings or splinters

Oak chips, oak shavings and oak splinters can be used interchangeably because they have comparable surface–to–weight ratios. If a carboy of wine will handle a cup of chips, it will probably accommodate a cup of shavings or splinters. That's not the case with oak sawdust, a cup of which would overwhelm 5 gallons.

In my experience, 5 gallons of white wine will absorb 1 –1$^1/_2$ cups of chips, splinters or shavings (approximately 1 to 1$^1/_2$ ounces) without becoming too heavily oaked. Five gallons of red wine will handle 2 to 3 cups, possibly up to one cup per gallon. Stuff the chips or splinters right into the carboy and test weekly to determine when to rack. There will be a pronounced oak flavor immediately after they are removed but the flavor will steadily diminish as the wine ages. It might totally disappear after 2 or 3 years.

If you have more than one carboy of wine, make one with no oak; when the two versions are compared, you might be less enthusiastic about oak as it covers up a lot of the fruit and subtle flavors. With one carboy not oaked, you also have the option of blending later in case you over–oaked. French oak imparts a more subtle but superior flavor in my opinion. But many winemakers prefer American oak, so it is a matter of personal preference.

Oak sawdust

Five gallons of white wine will *not* handle a cup or even $1/2$ cup of finely–ground oak sawdust. With granular oak, the best way is to make a small quantity of very concentrated oak–wine solution and use that to flavor the main body of wine. Put 8 ounces of sawdust in a half gallon or 2 liter jug plus $1/4$ tsp. of potassium metabisulfite and fill it with good quality white wine. Stir it very thoroughly and store it in the refrigerator for a week, shaking it occasionally.

After a week try some quantitative tests on small samples to determine how much of the oak–wine concentrate to add to the main batch. Pour 50 ml of the wine to be flavored into each of four or five different glasses, plus one that is not flavored. Using your pipet (or eye dropper, assuming 20 drops = 1 ml), flavor each glass as shown in following chart.

Glass #1	**No flavoring**
Glass #2	**.5 ml = 1%**
Glass #3	**1.0 ml = 2%**
Glass #4	**1.5 ml = 3%**
Glass #5	**2.0 ml = 4%**

Give them a few minutes to mix and decide which percentage is best for the wine in question. If the oak flavor seems too strong, double the wine volume to 100 ml. This sensory process is quite judgmental, so don't hesitate to call some friends in. Err on the conservative side because the only remedy for too much oak is blending, although the oak flavor will diminish markedly over the course of a year or two.

The excess concentrate can be stored in the refrigerator in a full bottle for a while as both the oak and the meta are preservatives. If you have both white and red wines to be flavored, the initial two quarts of oak flavored wine can be poured into a separate bottle and used for flavoring red wines. Refill the original bottle still containing the oak particulate, add more meta, and stir. After a week, you will have a weaker oak concentrate for use in the flavoring white wines.

Other brands of granular oak are undoubtedly available, but "Oak–Mor" is most commonly found and comes with instructions.

Oak staves

Some winemakers like oak staves, which are long slender sticks that can be dropped directly into the carboy for a few weeks to impart an oak flavor and then removed. When the flavor and tannins get leached out of the surface, the staves can be planed down to expose new wood. Staves also displace some of the volume in the carboy in case you find yourself a bit shy of 5 gallons after racking. Taste the wine every week or two, depending on how much surface area is exposed and how much oak flavor you want.

Toasted oak chips

This is a recent addition to the supplies available to the home winemaker. It adds a smoky flavor and increases the complexity and character of either a red or a white wine. Use it *very* sparingly — red wines will safely handle $1/_2$ cup per carboy and whites $1/_4$ cup. And not for too long. It's not the oak but the carbon that has the potential to overwhelm. Toasted oak can do wonders to perk up a wine that seems a little drab or lacking in complexity, particularly white wines. It also complements the natural flavors of pinot noir and zinfandel.

Oak barrels

I save this topic until last. Because in my opinion, oak barrels should be the very last thing on the home winemaker's mind! True, the great wines of the world have almost always been aged in oak. In addition to imparting a flavor pleasing to many people, oak cooperage allows a young wine to oxidize and mellow at a slow, controlled rate. It probably will not be long until you start thinking about aging or fermenting in oak.

Unfortunately, oak barrels are highly impractical for the home winemaker. First of all, the optimum surface–to–volume ratio is attained only with 55 gallon barrels, which requires the juice of almost 1,000 pounds of grapes to fill it. A 30–gallon barrel is usable, despite its dramatically higher surface–to–volume ratio. Although a wine could not be aged for 2 or 3 years in a 30–gallon barrel, as a winery might do in a 55–gallon barrel, it could be aged for a year or so and most of the benefits of oak aging attained. However, 30 gallons is still a lot of wine. And a reserve for topping up the barrel will be necessary as well. The problem with 15–gallon barrels is that the surface–to–volume ratio is so high as to limit the aging period so much that the desired oxidizing benefits of long term aging in cooperage will not be realized.

In addition to size considerations, oak barrels have to be monitored closely during aging and topped up religiously. It is easy for ethyl acetate, acetaldehyde or other organic defects to develop during any aging process which exposes the wine to air, however limited the exposure may be. Defects of this nature are unacceptable in even small amounts, and there is no remedy for it. Should one of these problems strike, the barrel would have to be reworked to remove the taint and avoid a repeat of the problem the next year (i.e., dismantled and the staves shaved).

The oak barrel enthusiast will also have the ongoing nuisance of maintaining the barrel between batches of wine. Water and SO_2 gas have to be added regularly to prevent drying out and/or molding. And after several seasons, the tannins and oak flavor will have been leached out of the oak. Your options then are to have the barrel reworked or to start adding oak flavor from an outside source, in the form of chips or staves. And all along, you will suffer from a lack of flexibility in that once used for a red wine, a barrel should not later be used for a white wine.

Oak barrels are a lot of work and greatly increase the chance of spoilage. There has probably been more wine spoiled and time and money wasted in oak barrel endeavors than any other aspect of home winemaking. If you still can't resist, at least be aware of what you are getting into. And get a good book on the care and maintenance of your cooperage.

Chapter Fifteen

CONCENTRATE KITS

he market for concentrate kits is booming! Modern food processing equipment and techniques have become highly sophisticated in recent years and enable musts to be condensed with minimal loss of flavor. Concentrate kits have little or none of the caramelized flavor associated with canned concentrates. The essence of the fruit is trapped as the base is gently reduced to the desired volume and then the essence is added back. Since modern processing techniques allow more of the grape to be retained, it makes sense nowadays to use higher fruit quality. Home winemakers can make enjoyable wines with concentrate kits any time of the year, no matter where they live. Very little equipment is needed, and the cost is reasonable. So the boom in Canada is quite understandable, and it is just underway in the United States.

There are numerous brands of these bagged and boxed products (see *Appendix G*), all marketed by Canadian companies as far as I am aware. The grapes come from all over the world — Italy, France, Chile, Argentina, Australia, California and Washington being the most common sources. Most are packaged to make 23 liters of finished wine, which is 5 Imperial gallons or 6 U.S. gallons. Those that have been concentrated the least are packaged in 15-liter boxes; you add 8 liters of water to bring the total to 23 liters. The next level down is packaged in 5 to 7 kilogram boxes to which considerably more water must be added to bring the total to 23 liters. Some companies also sell undiluted aseptic juice in 23-liter boxes. No water is added — just add yeast and ferment. These companies also market a variety of exotic specialty wines packaged to make smaller quantities of finished wine.

Bear in mind that concentrate kits are subject to the same old rule: the better the grapes, the better the wine. These producers have to line up their sources of supply and make commitments early in the summer, the same as wineries. Sometimes the grapes will be great and sometimes they will be below average. With the grapes coming from all over the world at different times of the year and typically being blended as well, it becomes impossible to conclude that one brand is better than another. Each will have some good ones in the pipeline at any given time and some not so good.

Once you understand the basic procedure of Chapter Two for fermenting white wines and Chapter Six for red wines, there is little more to be said about fermenting concentrate kits. All fermentations are basically the same. The kits come packaged with yeast, all the additives needed to ferment and clarify and instructions. You don't even need a crusher or press, just a primary fermenter, carboys, racking hose and stem, etc. Follow the directions, minimize the exposure to air, and you can expect 30 bottles of enjoyable wine.

You might find white wines from kits to be more difficult to clarify than wines from fresh grapes. The kits all come with one or two fining agents and directions which have undoubtedly been carefully tested. I have found Sparkolloid to be effective, but it takes two or three months to settle out, which is probably not consistent with the time frame of the concentrate kit fermenter. If you are not completely successful in clarifying your wine, don't worry about it as the residual haze is innocuous and will not affect the flavor.

The more concentrated the juice, the faster the wine will age. The 7-kg. boxes are marketed as "28-day" wines, and the 15-liter boxes as "6-week" wines. The aseptic juices are marketed as "six month" wines. Be aware that these are optimistic figures as the wines will all improve considerably after several additional months of aging.

In my opinion the future for concentrate kits looks very bright for home winemakers. I say this because the processing technology and equipment will continue to be refined. A few processors are starting to use spinning cone columns to reduce the musts, which has the potential to boost the quality even higher. With the large number of brands on the market, competition should keep prices down.

Here are notes on several of my fermentations.

"SIX-MONTH" ASEPTIC JUICE

23 Liters of "BURGUNDY"

LABEL: 23° B. sugar; 3.60 pH; 7.5 grams total acid; 78 parts per million sulfite. My saccharometer read 23° also; my Titret® ampule showed something less than 70 ppm sulfite; and the pH of the finished wine was 3.52.

DAY 1. Started a yeast starter by emptying a package of yeast in $1/2$ cup of warm water. Fifteen minutes later, when it was fully hydrated, I added 1 tsp. of sugar and a pinch of diammonium phosphate and set it aside. Poured entire 6 gallons, including pulp and sediment, into 7-gallon carboy rather than using a primary fermenter. Two hours later, I added the yeast starter over the surface of the must and emptied another package of the same yeast (Red Star Premier Cuvee) for good measure.

DAY 2. Fermentation underway. No air lock.

DAY 4. Vigorous fermentation. Sugar down to 1° B.

DAY 5. Saccharometer indicates sugar is -1° B. Still fermenting actively but much slower. Racked from the primary fermenter into 5-gallon carboy plus 3-liter jug. Topped with air locks.

DAY 11. Fell still.

DAY 14. Racked and sulfited. Final volume was almost 6 gallons. Set it outside to cold stabilize. After a month in the cool spring air, most of the solids will have settled out and the wine could be bottled. However, it has a sharp "bite" to the palate, as though a large amount of acid was added.

MONTH 2. Racked, adding $1/8$ tsp. of sulfite and 3 ounces of sugar to raise the residual sugar level to . 5%. The sugar made the wine more mellow but a bit more is needed to combat the artificial acid. Added another $1^1/2$ ounces of sugar, which seemed to add the desired balance.

MONTH 3. Bottled. The adjustments elevated this wine to what might be considered jug wine quality. The packaging did not indicate what is meant by "Burgundy," but I doubt that it contains any pinot noir.

Month 8. Quite to my surprise, it aged into a respectable red wine with some pinot noir qualities. At .75% RS it is too sweet, which was my error in judgement. For some reason it has a slight caramelized flavor.

"SIX-MONTH" ASEPTIC JUICE
23 Liters of "JOHANNISBERG RIESLING"
LABEL: 21.2° B. sugar; 3.00 pH; 8.3 grams total acid; 93 ppm sulfite.

DAY 1. Poured contents into 7-gal. glass carboy containing Steinberg lees from prior fermentation of gewurtztraminer. Add ½ tsp. DAP. Held overnight at room temp.

DAY 2. Fermentation underway. Took to garage to cold ferment.

4 WEEKS. Still fermenting but very slowly. Saccharometer reads negative. Set in warm room to ferment to completion. If the sugar had been higher initially, I might have stopped fermentation at 1% RS. But at 21° B., the alcohol level will only be 11%, so I need not be concerned about high alcohol and find it is easier just to add sugar back. Another option for adding a bit of residual sugar after fermentation would be the concentrated conditioners marketed by some of the concentrate kit companies, which is pure grape concentrate (fructose) with potassium sorbate to discourage renewed fermentation.

5 WEEKS. Fermentation is complete. Clinitest reads .1%. Removed the air lock and immediately replaced with a solid rubber stopper, wrapped in plastic wrap to give it a good seal. Set the carboy in the garage to settle for a week or two. There is almost a "gallon" of head space in the carboy, which is filled with almost pure carbon dioxide. It is imperative that the stopper not be removed until racking as air would get in.

6 WEEKS. The gross lees have settled out. Racked and sulfited with ¼ tsp. per 5 gallons. Have 5 gal. plus ½ gal. Sealed with rubber stopper and set outside to cold stabilize for a few weeks.

8 WEEKS. No further clearing. TA = .86%. Made Sparkolloid

slurry (7 tsp./5 gal. since it was quite cloudy) and racked, adding 17.5 g. of calcium carbonate (to lower TA by .14%). No sulfite. The wine cleared overnight. Much crystallization, which compacted the Sparkolloid lees.

9 WEEKS. TA = .74% — the carbonate lowered TA by .12% rather than .14%. This is a normal deviation. pH=3.2.

3 MONTHS. Racked, sulfited (¼ tsp.) and added 6 oz. of sugar to raise RS to 1%.

4 MONTHS. Wine is crystal clear. Bottled.

"SIX-WEEK" WINE KIT

JOHANNISBERG RIESLING

DAY 1. Mixed the bentonite in the blender per directions and put into primary fermenter (10-gal. can). Emptied the 15-liter foil bag into a 6-gallon (U.S.) pail. Rinsed the bag with warm water to dissolve the rest of the concentrate and sugar; added more warm water to fill the pail. Dumped the pail into the primary fermenter and stirred. Sugar tested 21° B., which is just right for a riesling. Rehydrated the Red Star Premier Cuvee yeast (Prise de Mousse) that came with the kit. After sprinkling the starter solution over the surface, I sprinkled another package of the same yeast in dry form directly onto the surface, for good measure. This wine was fermented at room temperature, but there is no reason it could not have been cold fermented over a longer period of time.

DAY 2. Fermentation underway.

DAY 4. Sugar down to 6° B.

DAY 8. Sugar at 2° B. Racked into a 5-gallon carboy and 1.5 liter jug and topped with air locks, discarding the bentonite and yeast lees. I could have fermented it to dryness at room temperature and added sugar back to sweeten it, but I chose instead to set it outside where the cool spring temperatures would slow down final fermentation.

DAY 14. Clinitest indicates that residual sugar is at 1%. Since this is the minimum level of residual sugar one would want in a wine of this type, I racked and sulfited (¼ tsp.) to stop fermentation. The yield was slightly over 5 gallons, the loss in volume being attributable to the use of bentonite. Left it outside so the gross lees could settle.

DAY 28. Very little clarification to date; the wine still looks viscous. Fined with Sparkolloid slurry at the rate of 1 tsp. per gallon. The directions say to add meta, sorbate and isinglass at this stage, but I chose Sparkolloid instead, intending to use the isinglass later if necessary.

MONTH 2. It needs a higher level of residual sugar for good balance. Racked, adding $1/8$ tsp. of sulfite and 6 ounces of table sugar to raise residual sugar from 1% to 2%. This seemed about right for my taste. The wine has cleared noticeably by now, though it will never be brilliant.

MONTH 3. Bottled. This is a pleasant semi-sweet riesling. It would not win any awards but most people would regard it as drinkable, if not enjoyable. I anticipate that it will improve somewhat with six months in the bottle.

MONTH 8. This has developed into a nice riesling without a trace of the "caramelized" flavor normally associated with a concentrate. The only shortcoming is that it is far too sweet for my palate. I should have left the residual sugar at 1%.

"SIX-WEEK" WINE KIT

ZINFANDEL

DAY 1. Emptied the 15-liter foil bag into a 6-gal. (U.S.) pail. Rinsed the bag with warm water to recover any remaining sugar and filled the pail with warm water. Poured into a 10-gal. primary fermenter and stirred. The pH tested 3.55 and total acid measured .69, which are good numbers. The sugar was low, however, at 18° B. Trusting the producer, I resisted the temptation to add more sugar. As a source of yeast and hopefully some added bouquet (and probably malolactic bacteria), I added approximately 1 gallon of skins of cabernet sauvignon (with the seeds shaken out using a nylon hops bag) — I had pressed a batch of cabernet sauvignon the same day.

DAY 2. Fermentation started. The cap will be punched down once or twice a day from now on.

DAY 6. Fermentation has come to a near standstill. Dipped the skins out with a stainless steel kitchen strainer and pressed by hand in a coarse nylon hops bag. Transferred the wine to glass containers, adding $1/2$ tsp. of yeast extract to encourage malolactic fermentation. (Concentrates can be put through malolactic fermentation but since they have been pasteurized, the bacteria must be added). Attached air locks and set in a small room warmed to 75 - 80° F. to encourage MLF. Have 5 gal. carboy + 1 gal. jug, both almost full.

DAY 9. Almost dry. Residual sugar tests .2% using Clinitest. Appears to be going through malolactic fermentation.

DAY 11. The continuing bubbles indicate secondary fermentation. I stir it occasionally with a slender dowel to disperse the nutrients on the bottom and speed the process up.

DAY 17. MLF appears to be complete — no more effervescence when stirred.

DAY 22. Chromatography confirms: no more malic acid remaining. TA = .67. Given the short time it took to complete MLF and the slight drop in total acid, this must had very little malic acid at the outset. Set outside to chill.

5 WEEKS. Racked and sulfited - $1/4$ tsp./ 5 gal. Some tartrate salts have already precipitated. Net yield was 5 gal. + 3 liters. Stored at room temperature for further settling.

10 WEEKS. Bottled. I cheated a little by adding $1/2$ tsp. of my Raspberry Liqueur (Appendix F) per bottle. TA = .66%. RS = .15%. pH = 3.49. Should be a very drinkable table wine in a few months.

TESTING PROCEDURES

Testing sugar content of the must

This is the easiest of all tests. All it requires is a special hydrometer known as a saccharometer and cylindrical jar to hold the sample. Take the reading from the bottom of the meniscus (refer to page 17). Note that pulp and solids suspended in the liquid will cause an artificially high reading. If you test right after pressing, deduct $1\frac{1}{2}$ ° B. as a rule of thumb. A better reading will result if the test sample is settled overnight and only the clear juice tested the next day. The degrees of sugar in a must is a rough indicator of the potential alcohol level — the actual alcohol level will be roughly half the Brix or Balling reading; e.g., 20° B. will result in a wine with 10% alcohol, more or less. A saccharometer will not read the actual alcohol level; a vinometer is required to do that.

The two most common scales for measurement of sugar are Brix and the older Balling scale. The two are essentially the same, except that Brix is standardized at a temperature of 20° C. (68° F.), whereas Balling is standardized at 15.5° C. (59° F.). The difference is not significant, so I treat the two scales as equals.

The calibrated temperature is marked on most hydrometers. If the temperature of the must is higher than the calibrated temperature, add approximately .25° B. to the reading for each 9° F.; if the actual temperature is below, deduct .25° B. from the reading for each 9° F.

Testing total acid

It's important to know the level of total acid of the must, starting at the time of the crush. Plan to do your own titration test when the grapes arrive, even if the vineyard gave you its reading. Your reading, even if less accurate, is the more important reference point for later measurements of the change in acid level after cold stabilization, during malolactic fermentation or after acid adjustment.

Acid titration tests require minimal equipment and can be purchased in kit form or assembled:

> Small beaker or jar
> .1N or .2N sodium hydroxide
> Distilled water
> Phenolphthalein
> Burette, or a 1 ml or 2 ml pipet, or an eye dropper

My preference is the 1 ml volumetric pipet, which is calibrated to .01 ml. A pipet is faster than a burette once you learn to control the rate of discharge. And it can be easily used in the field before harvest. If you have only an eye dropper available, one drop quite consistently equates to .05 ml. For most accurate results, the test sample, hydroxide and pipet or burette should all be at the same temperature. It is easiest to read the color change against a white background, such as sunlight reflected off white paper.

If you have .1N hydroxide, start with 1 ml of sample wine or must; if you have .2N hydroxide, start with a 2 ml of sample. When adding either hydroxide or wine sample, the excess should be wiped off the outside of the pipet. Add the sample to a beaker and then add one or two ounces of hot distilled water. Add a couple drops of phenolphthalein. Slowly drip hydroxide from the pipet into the beaker, swirling continuously, until you reach the endpoint, which will be indicated when the phenolphthalein turns faint pink and stays pink for 10 or 15 seconds. Multiply the ml of hydroxide used by .75, and the result is total acid in grams per liter, measured as tartaric. For example, if you started with 2 ml of sample wine or must and used .8 ml of .2N hydroxide, total acidity would be .6 (.8

ml X .75). Note that you would get the same result if you started with a 1 ml sample and used .1N hydroxide; .8 ml of hydroxide would have been used and acidity would be .6%.

A 50–ml burette is more work to set up and clean but requires less manual dexterity to use. The only difference in using a burette is the quantities of sample and hydroxide used. After getting it set up and clearing the air out of the channel so the hydroxide will flow freely, add 5 ml of wine or must sample to the beaker using a 5–ml pipet. Add 3 or 4 ounces of hot distilled water. Add 4 or 5 drops of phenolphthalein. Make note of the level of hydroxide in the burette, measuring from the bottom of the meniscus. Drip hydroxide in and swirl until it turns faint pink and holds for 15 seconds. Measure the new level in the burette, subtract to determine how many milliliters were required and multiply the result by .15. If 7 ml of .1N NaOH was needed to neutralize the 5–ml sample, total acidity is 1.05 (7 X .15). If you used .2N hydroxide, half as much hydroxide would have been required; you would get the same result by using a factor of .3 rather than .15.

In the case of red wines it is difficult to identify the titration endpoint because the phenolphthalein indicator is the same color as the sample. So you have to watch carefully. As the hydroxide is dripped in, the test solution will gradually turn lighter pink, then slightly gray and then clear. The endpoint will be indicated when it turns faint pink again. If you are titrating with a pH meter, the endpoint will occur at 8.2 pH.

Testing residual sugar

"Clinitest" tablets are a simple and reliable way to measure the level of unfermented sugar left in a wine, commonly referred to as residual sugar, or "RS." They come packaged with two color charts — 0 to 2% RS, and 0 to 5% RS. However, the older "Dextrocheck" chart, if you can find one, is better, as the color patches are on an ideal scale for testing of dry wines of 0% RS (blue) to 1% RS (orange). This scale is more convenient and accurate for dry wines than the charts packaged with Clinitest kits. Some wine supply shops or distributors have Dextrocheck charts available upon request. See a summary of the three charts on the following page.

In addition to Clinitest tablets, you will need a test tube and a

CHART	RS Range	No. of Drops	Volume
2 drop Clinitest	0–5%	2*	.1 ml
5 drop Clinitest	0–2%	5*	.25 ml
Dextrocheck	0–1%	10	.5 ml
* Plus 10 drops of water			

$1/2$ ml or 1 ml pipet (or at least an eye dropper). To test using the Dextrocheck chart, drop $1/2$ ml (10 drops) of the sample wine into the bottom of the test tube, drop a Clinitest tablet in and watch the color change from blue to green and possibly to orange as the reaction goes to completion. After the reaction stops, shake the tube a bit, wait a few seconds and compare the color against the chart. Using $1/2$ ml (10 drops) of test solution, dark blue will be zero RS on the Dextrocheck chart and orange will represent 1% RS.

If the reaction continued after the solution turned orange, the sample has more than 1% residual sugar. In that case you will need to dilute a sample and test again. Use .25 ml of sample wine (5 drops) and add .5 ml of water (10 drops) for additional liquid. Read the new result directly off the "5–drop" color chart that comes packaged with Clinitest to get the percentage RS. Or, double the results read off a Dextrocheck chart.

Clinitest tablets have many uses. They will confirm that your wine in the carboys fermented to completion; check before adding sulfite! They can be used to test residual sugar after sugar addition, but you have to wait a few weeks until the sucrose has been converted into fructose and glucose.

Clinitest tablets are indispensable if you want to stop fermentation at a predetermined level, such as 1%, before all sugar ferments. This will keep the alcohol level slightly lower and can be used to advantage where the grapes had excessive sugar that might result in an overly alcoholic wine. For example, if the grapes arrive at 26° Brix, the progress of fermentation can be monitored with Clinitest tablets and fermentation stopped at 1% residual sugar by racking, sulfiting and chilling. The alcohol level will be approximately .55% lower than it would be if fermented to dryness and sugar added back to raise RS to 1%. A slow fermenting yeast must be used in order to determine when to intervene and stop fermentation.

Paper chromatography

Chromatography is an easy way for the home winemaker to de-termine whether or not malolactic fermentation has gone to comple-tion. Fortunately, chromatography test kits are fairly inexpensive and easy to use. A kit will include the following essentials:

- Whatman paper (#1 or #20) — 8 X 10"
- capillary tubes
- capillary tube holder
- chromatography solvent
- wide mouth jar — 1 gal.
- malic & lactic acid reference solutions (0.3%)
- tartaric and citric acid reference solutions (0.3%) (optional)

The acid reference solutions can be purchased or else prepared by dissolving 300 mg of the acid in 100 ml of water. In addition, you will need a pencil and ruler and a stapler to fasten the paper into a cylinder.

Start by drawing a pencil line along the length of the Whatman paper, 1" from the bottom. Place dots at 1" intervals on the line. This is where the liquids will be spotted. A piece of paper will accommodate 3 acid samples and 7 wine samples marked in this manner. Identify each dot on the line with a pencil — "M" for malic, "L" for lactic, "T" for tartaric, etc. Also identify each wine sample to be spotted on the line and tested.

Now dip a capillary tube in the malic acid reference until it is about half full and touch it lightly to the "M" dot. You only want to release enough liquid to make a $1/4$" circle, so lift it the instant any liquid soaks into the paper. Do the same with the lactic acid reference and each other acid or wine sample, using a separate tube for each. Keep each circle as small as possible because that will result in a more clearly defined result. Replace each capillary tube in its ordered slot in the tube holder so they don't get mixed up.

Let the spots dry, which might take 10 or 15 minutes. Repeat the spotting process about 3 more times in the same places so that an intense acid mark is left at each dot on the line. Hopefully, none will be more than $1/4$", but there's no need to start over if a little too much liquid happens to escape the tube. It's just that the smaller and more concentrated the circles, the easier it will be to interpret the outcome when the paper dries.

Spot the paper four or five times. When the acid spots have dried, shape the paper into a cylinder and fasten it with staples. The edges should not overlap because then the acid spots would not move vertically. The pencil line along the base should line up where it meets.

Now pour about 2 ounces of the chromatography solution into the wide mouth jar. Be careful not to breathe the fumes. Stand the paper cylinder upright in the jar, pencil line at the bottom, and put the lid on. The solvent will gradually travel up the paper. Although nothing will be visible until the paper dries, the solvent takes the acid spots with it as it moves upward. Lactic acid travels most, followed by malic, citric and tartaric, in that order.

Leave the paper in the solution for 6 to 10 hours — until the solution has traveled almost to the top. It will take longer for Whatman #20 than #1. Then remove it and hang it to dry away from all chemical fumes. Spots will start to become visible after 2 or 3 hours of drying and will be quite conspicuous when the paper is completely dried. The Whatman paper becomes blue–green and the acid spots are yellow. The lactic reference acid will be closest to the top and the malic spot right below it. The tartaric reference spot will be nearest the pencil line.

Here's how you interpret the results (see illustration on following page). If the wine has not started malolactic fermentation, it will show only a malic spot at the same height as the malic acid reference spot, and no lactic spot, or a very faint lactic spot (see *Sample No. 1*). In the case of *Sample No. 2*, the lactic spot higher up with no malic spot indicates that it has gone completely through MLF — i.e., no malic remains, all of it having been converted to lactic. If it has both a lactic spot and a malic spot, then MLF is partially complete (see *Sample No. 3*). In the latter case, if the malic spot is bold and the lactic spot much lighter, then MLF is just underway, or maybe hasn't even started. If the lactic spot is bold and malic spot faint, then MLF is nearly complete. In this limited sense, the test is quantitative.

The chromatography solution can be poured back into the bottle after the test and re–used. The solvent will last a year or more. When the paper turns orange rather than blue–green, the solvent

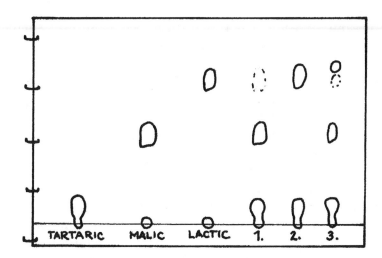

Chromatography Paper Test

is getting weak. Wash and dry your hands before handling the paper. Store the paper away from chemical fumes.

Note that if any artificial malic acid was added to the wine, as by using an acid blend, a malic spot will always appear. That's because artificial malic acid has a different chemical makeup from natural malic, and only half of the artificial version will be converted to lactic. Some malic will always remain, so chromatography is not a valid test.

Testing Free SO$_2$

At the levels discussed throughout this book, excess SO$_2$ will not be a problem. But curiosity or need to know the level of free SO$_2$ could arise. If so, sealed glass ampules marketed by Chemetrics as Titrets® are the most practical way a home winemaker can accurately test for free SO$_2$ in solution. Titrets® could be used to ascertain the level of free SO$_2$ at bottling time. White wines should have 20–30 ppm of free SO$_2$ when bottled and red wines 40–50 ppm. Or if you had to give a must an extra heavy dose of meta due to sunburn or bunchrot and later wanted to induce MLF, Titrets® can be used to check the level of free SO$_2$ before adding the ML starter.

The instructions with each package of ten vials are quite good. Push the flexible tube over the slender tippet of the ampule until it reaches the white line. Then break the tippet. Stick the end in the sample and draw some sample wine up by pinching the glass bead in the tube. The solution will instantly turn dark blue but will gradually lighten as more sample is added. When it has only a touch of blue, the endpoint has been reached. Invert the ampule and read the free SO_2 level as parts per million. Chemetrics markets a "Titrettor" for pinching the tube and letting sample in, but pinching the bead with thumb and forefinger gives you more control.

The Ripper method (i.e., Titrets) will give a fairly accurate reading of free SO_2 but could be off by 10-20 ppm. If you are a serious winemaker and highly concerned about free SO_2, you might want to invest in the equipment to test by the vacuum aspiration method, which is superior. The equipment shouldn't cost more than $100.

Note that if you happened to use too much meta by mistake, the excess can be neutralized with 3% hydrogen peroxide of the ordinary drug store variety. The addition of .7 ml per gallon will lower the sulfite level by approximately 10 parts per million. Make sure it is fresh as peroxide is unstable and has limited shelf. The effect should first be tested on a sample before treating the main batch of wine.

TROUBLE SHOOTING

Difficulty initiating fermentation

If there is no sign of fermentation after 36 hours, something is amiss. If the sulfite was kept within limits, difficulty in initiating fermentation is usually the result of a temperature that is too low. If the must temperature was below 60°, the temperature should be raised to 65 – 70°. If you cannot raise the room temperature or bring the must inside, you can drop in a couple of plastic milk containers filled with warm water. Or dip out a couple of buckets of the must, stand them in hot water and dump them back into the fermenter when warmed.

If temperature is not the problem, rack or pour the must into another container, aerating it as much as possible in the process. Or, use a 12–volt electric air pump, hose and racking stem to bubble air through it for a few seconds. Add 1/2 tsp. of diammonium phosphate or yeast nutrient per 5 gallons if not previously added and sprinkle more yeast on the surface if you are using a dry yeast. Keep the temperature up and it should start.

Stuck fermentation

On rare occasions active fermentation will slow prematurely and eventually stop before all the sugar has been converted to alcohol.

This is most likely to occur after a fermenting must which is nearly dry has been subjected to cold temperatures for an extended period of time. Fermentation will always stop when the temperature drops low enough. And it will always start up again when the temperature is raised. The question is whether it will resume with enough vigor to go to completion. The yeast might not have enough nitrogen stored up to ferment to dryness.

If fermentation does not rebound to a healthy rate after the temperature is raised to 70°, rack and aerate the wine, adding yeast extract. Add another $1/2$ tsp. of diammonium phosphate (D.A.P.). or a balanced yeast food (which will be predominantly D.A.P.). It would also be advisable to re–inoculate with a fresh starter of a vigorous and alcohol–tolerant yeast, such as Prise de Mousse and to maintain room temperature.

If this does not work, the only choice left is to build a new yeast starter solution and start "doubling." Get a small volume of fresh grape juice, preferably of the same grape variety. If you have ten gallons of stuck must, for example, two to four quarts of fresh starter should suffice. If you cannot locate the same grape variety, use a compatible variety that would be acceptable for blending. If that is not possible, use two quarts of Thompson seedless grape juice. Since the new starter will constitute up to ten per cent of the volume, the acidity and pH of the starter should not be radically different from that of the stuck wine.

The object is to cultivate a new yeast starter with a vigorous and alcohol–tolerant yeast and once it is fermenting actively, to add an equal volume of the stuck must. If you have two quarts of fresh starter solution, add two quarts of the stuck must. When this enhanced volume is fermenting actively, then double it again by adding four quarts of the stuck must. Then double again, etc.

Activate the yeast and begin the starter the night before, using D.A.P. or a balanced yeast food. Start the doubling process the next morning or as soon as the starter is fermenting vigorously. This project should be closely attended so that the time lag from start to finish is minimized. It should be completed in a matter of hours, not days, because fully half of the stuck must will be added at the last doubling. By that time the unfermented sugar will have dropped to a very low level, and the environment will be much less conducive for fermentation.

A stuck fermentation can sometimes be reactivated but often not. The sooner it is detected and corrective measures taken, the more likely success in restarting fermentation. It is also more difficult to re–initiate fermentation if the wine is almost dry. If these steps are not successful in restoring a vigorous fermentation, start planning what to do with a sweet wine, such as bottling sweet or blending with next year's dry wine.

Hydrogen sulfide

Hydrogen sulfide, or H_2S, smells like rotten eggs and can be the beginning of *major* problems. Hydrogen sulfide is most likely to be encountered with grapes that had excess sulfur on the skins at the time of crushing, although there are other causes, too. The sooner the problem is discovered and addressed, the easier it will be to correct and the less the quality of the wine will suffer. If left to run its course, what starts out as hydrogen sulfide will convert into mercaptans, which are harder to deal with and then into disulfides, which are even more challenging. The chemical remedy for dealing with mercaptans/disulfides in an advanced stage is beyond the scope of this book as it involves qualitative sensory tests using cadmium sulfate, which is highly poisonous, and using ascorbic acid to convert the disulfides back to mercaptans so that copper sulfate will work. The advice that follows assumes the problem has been detected and addressed early on and has not progressed to the disulfide stage.

If H_2S is detected early in fermentation, the fermenting wine should be racked off the lees and pulp immediately and a balanced yeast food or diammonium phosphate added at the rate of $1/_2$ tsp. per 5 gallons. This may solve the problem. If the smell returns, rack it a second time and a third time, but omitting the chemicals. The object of racking is to separate and discard the pulp on the bottom of the carboy as it contains most of the H_2S–generating constituents. If H_2S is not generated until late in fermentation, the D.A.P. probably will not help. But two or three rackings still might take care of the stink.

As soon as Clinitest confirms that fermentation is complete, the wine should be racked off the lees. Extended aging on the lees is an invitation to post–fermentation conversion of hydrogen sulfide compounds into mercaptans. So rack and sulfite soon after the wine has fallen still, even if the odor has disappeared.

Copper should not be added during fermentation, but it is safe and advisable to add minute amount of copper after it has fermented to completion. Add .15 ml of copper sulfate (1% $CuSO_4 \cdot 5H_2O$) per gallon, which will add .1 ppm of copper. It would also be good practice to fine with Sparkolloid at this racking, which will eliminate more of the impurities. Stopper it up and set it in a cool place.

As long as the stopper stays seated, the problem is probably under control. If the stopper starts popping out, the hydrogen sulfide compounds are being converted into mercaptans. Promptly rack again, but this time the wine should be racked into an air–free atmosphere if possible — i.e., displace the air with CO_2, argon or nitrogen before racking. Add another .15 ml of copper sulfate. Even with two small additions of copper, you will be well under the FDA limit for residual copper of .2 parts per million.

The odds are high that these measures, taken promptly as needed, will solve the problem. Some of the compounds may have progressed to the mercaptan stage but none to the disulfide stage. So the rackings and copper addition should deal with it.

Note that copper could also be added by trickling the wine down 12– or 14–gauge copper wires projecting out of the carboy/funnel. Use about 3 wires as very little copper exposure is needed or desired. I prefer copper sulfate because then you know how much copper is being added.

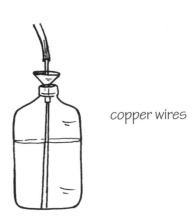

copper wires

Off Odors And Flavors

Browning in a finished wine is a sign of oxidation. Excessive exposure to air could have resulted from fermenting too long in an open fermenter before transferring to carboys or from storage in carboys that were not filled to the top. Fining with PVPP (and sulfiting, of course) after the fact might help reduce the browning.

If your wine has a vinegary taste, the flaw is acetic acid. Since some of this volatile acid is always formed during primary fermentation, it will be present in low levels in virtually every wine and is not objectionable at low levels. However, at some higher level, which varies from one palate to the next, it becomes a flaw. The acetic acid resulting from fermentation will usually not rise to that level. But if the ever-present acetobacter are given enough time in the presence of oxygen, they will convert ethanol into acetic acid and very likely ruin the wine.

If your wine tastes vinegary and exposure to air was not the cause, perhaps the grapes were overripe or had too much bunch rot or the pH was high and it was fermented too warm. If a must is fermented warm without sulfiting first, spontaneous malolactic fermentation might have started with one of the undesirable strains that generates acetic acid.

As alcohol is oxidized, the first stage is acetaldehyde. Acetaldehyde is also present in all wines and at low levels contributes to complexity. At higher levels it will make a wine seem "flabby" or "flaccid;" i.e., lacking in fruit and varietal characteristic and seemingly sweet. If ethanol is oxidized further, acetic acid will result and finally ethyl acetate. Ethyl acetate is an ester having a most unpleasant odor, like nail polish remover or airplane glue. It is to me the vilest of all organic flaws, although I know people who seem not to detect it or be bothered by it. There is no cure for ethyl acetate in even the smallest amount.

Note that for the most part, there is no satisfactory "cure" for any of the organic defects discussed above. Prevention in the form of a proper pre-fermentation acid level (at least .6% TA), sulfite and air avoidance is by far the best remedy. It is natural to think that by blending the flaw will be diminished. Depending on the problem, it usually does not work that way — normally the blend to be just as flawed as the problem wine. If you have one of these organic defects and sufficient volume of wine to make it worth the effort, consult with someone locally who can give you some perspective, as these problems are difficult to diagnose and treat. A heavy dose of sulfite (100 ppm) may be the best palliative. After that, you could consider trying to mask some of the defect with oak flavoring or a higher level of residual sugar.

Finished wines that have a "pruney" flavor were usually made from over-ripe grapes with high sugar and were fermented too hot. A pruney flavor right after fermentation will diminish with time but will not always disappear. If your grapes have abnormally high sugar, keep the temperature in the 70s if you can; don't let it rise to the high 80s. Be sure to sort out all raisined and spoiled grapes before crushing.

Generating Carbon Dioxide

Air is the number one enemy of white wines. Even by keeping the number of rackings to an absolute minimum, the wine will suffer some damage from air contact. However, if the number of rackings is kept to a minimum and the wine is bottled young, the loss in quality will be so minimal as to be undetectable. But if more than about three rackings become necessary, or if you end up having to rack in the summer or fall when the wine is not only more mature but also warmer, or if you had problems with microbial activity after fermentation finished, it would be good procedure to displace the air in the empty carboy with an inert gas, such as CO_2, nitrogen or argon, before racking into it.

This is easy for beermakers with a CO_2 tank and regulator — just fill the carboy with gas right before you rack and the gas, being heavier than air, will settle to the bottom and protect the wine as it flows in. Argon would be even better than CO_2. It is more expensive but you use so little of it that the cost per fill is nominal.

Home winemakers without the luxury of a CO_2 tank can accomplish the same result by fermenting corn sugar solely for the purpose of generating CO_2. Here's how. Dissolve the corn sugar at the rate of 20 ounces per gallon of hot water and add a generous amount of D.A.P. or last year's yeast food. Cane or beet sugar could be used instead, but corn sugar will ferment more willingly. Mash some fruit or vegetables to add nutrients for the yeast; even cucumbers, green tomatoes or carrot shavings will work! Use a vigorous yeast strain, such as Prise de Mousse, and you will soon have a "CO_2 pot," as I call it. If you have other wine fermenting in a carboy, you don't even need to bother with sugar water; just channel the CO_2 from the fermenting carboy.

Channel the gas into the new carboy for an hour or two before racking using a $1/2$" vinyl hose attached to a two–piece, straight–tube air lock. Wrap a piece of aluminum foil around the neck of the carboy while the CO_2 is flowing in. Several carboys can be readied in the days before the racking — just add the $1/4$ tsp. of meta–water, displace the air with CO_2 and stopper them until racking day.

Don't feel that you have to always displace air before racking or run out and buy a tank and regulator. It is not necessary to displace the air as long as the number of rackings is minimized. And it is not necessary at the first racking, when the wine is saturated with carbon dioxide and has little capacity to absorb oxygen. Consider it only when the number of rackings becomes excessive, or when having to rack during the heat of summer or late in the life of the wine. Or after having experienced microbial activity, when exposure to oxygen should be avoided.

Displacing the air is an extra step. And it requires an additional supply of empty carboys. But it is an inexpensive way for the home winemaker to minimize oxygen absorption under conditions where the wine might otherwise suffer noticeable loss in quality.

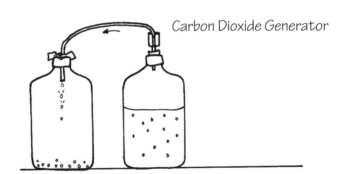

Carbon Dioxide Generator

Grape Varieties

There are hundreds of different grape varieties; the list that follows contains only the more common types, grouped by species.

VITIS VINIFERA

Vitis vinifera is rightfully regarded as the elite species for winemaking. The better ones have no equal. In addition to California and the Pacific Northwest, *vinifera* acreage is increasing in the Northeast, Mid-Atlantic regions of the U.S. and in parts of Canada.

Red vinifera

CABERNET SAUVIGNON. The blue berries of this premier wine grape variety are very small. The resulting high skin-to-juice ratio produces a wine that is very dark, intense and tannic. Since the skins are tough and the clusters are loose and easily aerated, this variety will survive bad weather before harvest with minimum susceptibility to mildew or bunch rot. Although it takes a fair amount of heat to ripen Cabernet Sauvignon to the point where the wine will have the classic black currant overtones, the grape will grow in cooler climates and produce a respectable red wine. However, if not sufficiently ripened or if the canopy is so heavy as to restrict aeration and sunlight, the wine will have a vegetative bouquet and flavor. Cabernet Sauvignon buds later than Merlot and is less vulnerable to late spring frosts. The juice is clear when first pressed and makes a wonderful rosé — if you can bear to part with a full-bodied wine!

MERLOT. The plump black grapes of Merlot make a soft, fruity wine very deserving of its current boom in popularity. Merlot is lower in acid, ripens about a week earlier and ages faster than Cabernet Sauvignon. It also tolerates cool, damp soils better than Cabernet Sauvignon, but its thin-skinned berries are more subject to mildew and rot. When Merlot and Cabernet Sauvignon are blended, the result is often better than either one alone. The crop set is erratic and is adversely affected by spring rains right after budding.

CABERNET FRANC. This very cold-hardy red grape does very well in parts of the Northeast United States, Long Island and Ontario's Niagara peninsula. Like Merlot, Cabernet Franc is lighter in color and tannin and ripens earlier than Cabernet Sauvignon. It has traditionally been used in Bordeaux for blending with Cabernet Sauvignon and is gaining in popularity in the United States, both as a straight varietal and for blending. It also blends very well with Merlot. Cabernet Franc tends to over-produce unless the yield is restricted.

PINOT NOIR. Pinot Noir is the most difficult variety to grow and to ferment. Almost never do the results equal the fine red Burgundies by which Pinot Noir wines are inevitably judged. However, with ripe grapes, a very good red wine can be expected. The grape is inherently low in tannin and light in color, and the color diminishes further as the wine ages and bottle sediment develops.

For a lighter wine that emphasizes the grape's delightful fruitiness, try "cold-soaking" for several days after crushing but before fermentation. This is widely believed to produce a wine with softer flavors, more fruit and a deeper, more stable color. You could also ferment 10 - 20% whole clusters in the must to emphasize the fruit. By pressing early, say at 5° B., you would avoid the harsher tannins that would be extracted at higher alcohol levels.

For a bigger bodied wine that will take longer to age and have less fruit but more complexity, crush and de-stem rigorously to macerate the grapes as much as possible. With fully ripe grapes, ten per cent of the stems could be returned to the must before primary fermentation to increase tannin. It could also be put through extended maceration but this will further reduce the fruit.

It is usually necessary to put Pinot Noir through malolactic fermentation as a means of getting total acidity down into the desired range. A limited exposure to toasted oak improves this wine in my opinion.

The many clones of Pinot Noir all tend to have tight clusters and tender skin, which makes them susceptible to mildew and bunch rot if damp weather sets in just before harvest. To hedge against this possibility, you might want to pick some at 18 - 20° B., as Pinot Noir makes an excellent sparkling wine. Press without crushing first, and the juice will be white. This juice is excellent for blending with white varieties.

SYRAH a/k/a Shiraz. Serious California wineries are starting to bottle Syrahs that rival the fine wines of Hermitage and Côte-Rôtie, albeit with more fruit and lower tannin. At its best, syrah makes a big, spicy and complex red wine that takes many years to mellow. I prefer it blended with other red varieties. It ripens a little earlier than Cabernet Sauvignon.

ZINFANDEL. When the yield per acre is limited, Zinfandel makes a spectacular, spicy full-bodied wine. "White Zinfandel," so popular with the American public, is fermented from heavily-cropped central valley grapes. Serious winemakers will want grapes originating farther north in California, where cooler weather will allow for slower, more even ripening. When fermenting overripe Zinfandel, be sure to cull out those that are raisined and carefully monitor the fermentation temperature to avoid a "pruney" flavor. Try to keep the wine temperature below 80° F. during fermentation. It's okay to leave around .5% of residual sugar in this red wine, as the commercial wineries often do.

White vinifera

CHARDONNAY. It should come as no surprise that the grape that gives us the great Meursaults and Montrachets of Burgundy is so widely planted throughout the world. It is quite hardy and adapts to a wide range of climates. The problem with Chardonnay is that it is a challenge to grow and a challenge to ferment. Unless well ripened, it has little inherent varietal characteristic. The quality of the wine falls off rapidly as the tonnage surpasses the optimum yield per acre, which will vary from one region to the next. Its tight clusters are not easily aerated, making it quite susceptible to mildew and bunch rot in damp weather.

It is best in my opinion to soak Chardonnay grapes on the skins for 24 hours before pressing and fermenting. I am partial to cold fermentation with Steinberg yeast, but wineries typically ferment with more vigorous yeast strains at 65° (or start lower and let the temperature rise after the sugar drops below 10° B.). Although I confess to liking the buttery flavor that results from malolactic fermentation, I have mixed emotions about MLF because it eliminates so much of the fruit flavor. It also seems to make the wine more difficult to clarify. When I do opt for MLF, which is usually when total acidity is high, I keep the temperature fairly warm and stir the lees two or three times a week. This imparts the maximum yeasty flavor in addition to promoting MLF. (Note that if you want to keep the temperature abnormally warm during MLF, avoid the vigorous yeasts; otherwise, autolysis is likely, where the yeast cannibalize each other after the sugar is gone and leave a bad flavor). Sometimes I flavor a Chardonnay with French oak and sometimes not, since the oak flavoring masks some of the fruitiness

SAUVIGNON BLANC. The vines of Sauvignon Blanc are very vigorous and if not pruned to give the grapes some air and sunlight, the grapes will develop an overwhelming grassy quality. Going to the opposite extreme, many U.S. wineries maximize exposure to air and sunlight by canopy management and put the wine through malolactic fermentation as well. The resulting wine will more easily pass for a Chardonnay than a classic Sauvignon Blanc that goes so well with seafood. Sauvignon Blanc is often blended with Semillon and marketed as "Fumé Blanc."

SEMILLON. Semillon is one of the most widely planted white grapes in the world. It is the basic grape of white Bordeaux and of Sauternes (it is very prone to *Botrytis cinerea*, the "noble rot"). Semillon is commonly blended with Sauvignon Blanc to round out the flavor of the latter and with Chardonnay as an extender. With the right grapes, semillon will make a serious white wine capable of long-term aging.

PINOT GRIS. This relative of Pinot Noir is known as Tokay in Alsace and as Pinot Grigio in Italy, where it produces an excellent, dry white wine with a pleasing lemony quality. In the United States it can make a high quality white wine rivaling Chardonnay or Sauvignon Blanc in quality. If well ripened, Pinot Gris wines have a pleasant spicy quality; but if allowed to get over-ripe, the grapes tend to lose character and will turn red if left to hang too long. Pinot Gris tends to have high acid and low pH, even at high sugar levels. Since this variety is also quite low in varietal characteristic, malolactic fermentation can often be used to good advantage, to add some body to the wine. Pinot Gris is less susceptible to mildew and bunch rot and ripens earlier than Chardonnay.

JOHANNISBERG RIESLING, a/k/a White Riesling. This is a great one for home winemakers to ferment! It is more widely available than other varieties because the vines are very hardy and will thrive in cooler climates, such as the northeast United States and southeast Canada. It does extremely well in New York. Even if harvested early and sugar added, it will make a nice wine with the distinctive riesling aroma. It can be made dry or sweet or in between and is a good grape for sparkling wine. Riesling can be left hanging longer than other varieties because the berries are highly resistant to frost. If healthy grapes are left to hang, with luck they might become infected with *Botrytis cinerea*, and you will have the makings for a delicious sweet wine! Note that in hot climates riesling ripens too quickly and loses much of its quality.

GEWURTZTRAMINER. I have never figured out why Gewurtztraminer lacks commercial appeal because they can be such fine wines — perhaps the majority of the buying public have never had a good one. Gewurtztraminer is similar to Riesling in that it excels in cool climates and makes a good dry wine as well as sweet. The berries are small and pink and the wine is full-bodied, aromatic and easy to recognize. The acid level tends to fall rapidly as Gewurtztraminer ripens, so tartaric acid often must be used to raise acidity.

FRENCH HYBRIDS

There are dozens of different French hybrids, interspecific hybrids and French-native American hybrids under cultivation in the Midwest, Southeast, Northeast regions of the United States and in parts of Canada. They generally were selected over *vitis vinifera* varieties for their greater cold hardiness, tolerance of humidity, and/or resistance to fungal diseases, rot, pests and mildew. They are superior to *vitis labrusca* because they are less foxy and make far better wines. However, if allowed to over-ripen, some hybrids will develop a "cotton candy" and foxy flavor. It is critical that they be harvested at the right level of ripeness. Commercial wineries often deal with these unwanted flavors by heat treatment and/or carbonic maceration. Avoid extensive skin contact during fermentation of red hybrids; plan to press as soon as the wine has developed sufficient color.

Hybrids for the most part are diminishing in importance as more is learned about cultivating *vinifera* varieties in different locales. The white hybrids are generally of higher quality than the reds.

Here is a list of the better hybrids for winemaking:

White French hybrids

CAYUGA WHITE. Cayuga White is a relatively new cross which is productive, disease-resistant and very versatile. It can be fermented into a fruity, off-dry white wine or, with oak aging, into a more complex, dry table wine. It's also good for sparkling wine. Don't let it get too ripe or it will develop some foxiness.

VIDAL BLANC, a/k/a Vidal. With fully ripened grapes Vidal blanc will make a good fruity, floral wine reminiscent of riesling — dry, semi-sweet or sweet. It is popular in Canada as a late-harvest dessert wine. It is a heavy producer and needs a long growing season, so cluster thinning is required.

SEYVAL BLANC. This is a good white hybrid of long standing. It ripens early and can be fermented in various styles — crisp, dry, fruity or put through MLF for a more complex wine. Seyval Blanc is productive and does well in cool climates but is very susceptible to bunch rot.

VIGNOLES, a/k/a Ravat. Vignoles ripens to a high sugar level while retaining high acidity, making it an excellent choice for late-harvest and ice wines. It can also be made into a dry white table wine. In addition to its versatility, Vignoles is a very hardy and is seldom affected by frosts since it has a late budbreak. Its principal drawback is that very compact clusters make it highly susceptible to bunch rot.

TRAMINETTE. This is a new variety developed at the NYS Agricultural Experimental Station by Cornell University which, according to all reports, should not be stigmatized as a "hybrid." It is just starting to become commercially available and is expected to establish itself quickly because the wine, similar to Gewurtztraminer, is high quality, has a good balance of sugar, acid and pH, and ages well. The vines are cold hardy and the berries quite resistant to rot and mildew.

Red French hybrids

CHAMBOURCIN. This is a relatively new hybrid that makes a full-bodied wine of good quality when the grapes ripen fully. The wine is fruity and aromatic, slightly herbaceous. Due to high yields per acre, it should be cluster thinned. Chambourcin will tolerate humidity and is cold hardy but is late ripening and needs a long growing season.

CHANCELLOR, a/k/a Seibel 7053. Though not quite as well regarded as Chambourcin, this transplant from the Rhone Valley makes good reds and rosés. It is moderately hardy. Clusters should be thinned to promote ripening. It is susceptible to mildew.

BACO NOIR, a/k/a Baco No. 1. Makes an intense red wine with some aging potential, despite low tannin. It is very vigorous but disease-prone and frost-prone due to early budbreak.

MARECHAL FOCH, a/k/a Foch. This winter-hardy hybrid has been around a long time. It ripens very early and its black berries produce a fruity red wine with some Burgundian qualities. It lends itself to carbonic maceration.

VITIS LABRUSCA

The wines made from *vitis labrusca* tend to have a "foxy" quality which experienced wine drinkers find objectionable. The riper the grape, the more pronounced the foxiness; so with these varieties, it is better to harvest a little too green than too ripe. However, if picked green they will be quite acidic. As a result, 3 or 4 parts of the must is commonly diluted with one part of water sweetened to about 20° B. with table sugar. Foxiness is also reduced by pressing immediately after crushing to minimize skin contact. It's a good idea to line the press basket with fiberglass mesh as the tough slipskins make pressing difficult. Pressing is made easier and the yield increased if pectic enzyme is used.

DELAWARE. The small pink berries of Delaware ripen early and are used to make sparkling wines in particular, but also dry, sweet and ice wines. It has a spicy, musky aroma and is probably the least foxy *labrusca*.

CATAWBA. Since it is quite foxy, these pink grapes are usually converted into white or pink dessert wines, of which the quality can be quite good. It is also used for super-sweet ice wines. The grapes are acidic and the wine will improve somewhat with age. It requires a long growing season.

NIAGARA. This white grape is quite foxy and aromatic. It is usually used to make a sweet version, but sometimes dry. The vines are vigorous and productive.

CONCORD. This is probably the least desirable *labrusca*, due to foxiness and harshness. It has high acid and is best made into a sweet wine.

Fermentation Notes

CABERNET SAUVIGNON
MALOLACTIC FERMENTATION
EXTENDED MACERATION

DAY 1. Crushed and destemmed 130# Cabernet Sauvignon. Tested 25° B. right after pressing, with pulp (probably about 24° B. without pulp); .83 TA; 3.43 pH. Sulfited @ ¼ tsp./5 gal. of volume; used pectic enzyme to hasten maceration. Added 1 tsp. of diammonium phosphate. Soaked overnight on skins. Grapes had little flavor.

DAY 2. Brought into warm room — used space heater to raise ambient temperature to 75-80° F. Inoculated with Pasteur Red starter solution sprinkled over surface. Fermentation was visible in a few hours.

DAY 3. Cap starts forming.

DAY 4. Deep cap. Since malolactic fermentation is desired with the acid being .83, this is the time to add ML starter & yeast extract. Note that it is normal for the temperature of a fermenting wine to run 5 - 15° above ambient temp. This is due to the heat generated by fermentation. You want the fermenting wine temp. to run up to 80 - 90° for two or three days during active fermentation in order to maximize extraction of flavors and color. Monitor with a floating thermometer or an indoor-outdoor digital thermometer and don't let it exceed 90°. Wine must be punched down at least twice a day.

DAY 10. Cap is greatly diminished. Unfermented sugar is slightly over 1%, per Clinitest. Room temp. and wine temp. are almost the same now at 75°. It could be pressed now, but I am putting this batch through extended maceration. Covered the cap with a layer of plastic wrap after punching down, to keep air away.

DAY 11. Punching down once a day now and covering with plastic wrap.

DAY 14. Wine is dry. Clinitest turns slightly yellow but the red pigment is so overwhelming that a reliable reading on residual sugar is not possible. Hopefully, the slight bubble formation is a sign of malolactic fermentation, but it might just be trapped CO_2 escaping. Tastes bitter and tannic.

DAY 16. Still some bubbles escaping. Cap floating on surface, so no need to punch down. Wine mellowed; has spectacular flavor and fruit — should be excellent wine!

DAY 17. Wine bitter again.

DAY 20. Ran chromatography test: malolactic fermentation is complete. Pressed lightly and sulfited — $1/4$ tsp./ 5 gal. Ended up with 5 gal. + 3 gal. + 3 liters, some of which will be lost as pulp and lees at the next racking. Placed outside to cold stabilize (optional with red wines) and clear. The wine is bitter and tannic again but has an immense amount of fruit. In hindsight, I should have racked on Day 16, as it was sweeter then, but an extra 4 days on the skins will not make much difference.

5 WEEKS. Wine has good color and clarity. Tastes tannic. pH = 3.65.

9 WEEKS. First racking. Although none of the stoppers had popped, there was a mild hydrogen sulfide odor. So I aerated during racking by trickling the wine down the side of the carboy and added .1 part per million copper sulfate (.15 ml/gal. of 1% $CuSO_4 \bullet 5H_2O$). Some of the H_2S might have converted to mercaptans but not to disulfides, given the short time on the lees and faintness of the odor. Although there should not be a problem with this wine, this is a good example of the importance of monitoring a wine during the days and weeks immediately after fermentation ceases. The more pulp and sediment, the greater the risk of problems. Had I left it unattended for a few more weeks, the H_2S

would have been converted to mercaptans and possibly disulfides. Have 5 gal. + 2.8 gal. + 1.5 liters. TA tests .73.

16 WEEKS. TA tests .735% and will have to be lowered chemically. Have 5 gal. + 3 gal. The small carboy is earmarked for blending with next fall's merlot and will not be adjusted now. Racked 5 gal., adding 12.5 g. calcium carbonate (to lower TA by .1%). No sulfite. May have to add a bit more at the next racking.

17 WEEKS. TA = .62%. Has good flavor but not much bouquet.

18 WEEKS. TA = .69%. pH = 3.88 — the carbonate raised the pH far more than I wanted or expected. Since the pH is already higher than I would like, I will live with high total acidity. It does not tastes acidic.

5 MONTHS. Racked, added 2 cups American oak chips to 5 gal. carboy and 50 ppm sulfite.

8 MONTHS. Racked both carboys,.

10 MONTHS. Bottled 5-gal. carboy. Due to the high pH, I added 75 ppm of sulfite at bottling. Holding 3-gal. for blending.

CHARDONNAY
COLD FERMENTATION
MALOLACTIC FERMENTATION

210 pounds of Chardonnay, 21.5° B. at pressing, acid and pH not tested. Grapes had some bunch rot from recent rains, which I sorted/cut out with as much patience as I could muster. Grapes taste sweet but not much flavor. With sugar at this relatively low level, the acid level will be high, and malolactic fermentation looks like a good way to lower it.

DAY 1. Crushed and added $1/4$ tsp. sulfite per 5 gal. of volume. Covered with plastic wrap and soaked on skins for 24 hours to pick up additional flavor.

DAY 2. Pressed, giving the must another half dose of meta (1/8 tsp./5 gal.). Sugar dropped to 21° B. after pressing (because pressed juice is slightly lower in sugar than the free-run juice tested yesterday). Inoculated with Montrachet yeast starter. Must has peculiar odor.

DAY 4. Still no sign of fermentation (wine has been in cold garage). Added some yeast lees which was siphoned from a different batch of wine containing Steinberg yeast. Steinberg is active at lower temperatures.

DAY 5. Fermentation under way. Could be either Montrachet or Steinberg — it's probably Steinberg, but it doesn't matter.

DAY 6. Fermentation very active. Transferred to carboys, 3/4 full; topped with air lock.

DAY 13. Fermenting slowly.

4 WEEKS. Fermenting slowly.

5 WEEKS. Fermenting slowly; still tastes fairly sweet. Combined carboys. Note that with Steinberg yeast it would take several weeks for the last 1% of the sugar to ferment. So I brought it to room temp. to ferment it to total dryness faster. Fermentation picked up as soon as the temp. started to rise.

6 WEEKS. Being held at approx. 70° F. Fermenting very slowly.

7 WEEKS. One carboy is still, the other ferments slowly.

8 WEEKS. Both carboys are still. Raised ambient temp. to 75-80°. The next day I stirred in 1 tsp. yeast extract per carboy and malolactic starter (Chr. Hansen *Viniflora Oenos*). Stirred up lees and replaced air lock. The wine will be maintained at 75-80° and the nutrients stirred up with a slender dowel until malolactic fermentation is complete. MLF will lower total acid, and the diacetyl produced as a byproduct of MLF will give the wine a distinctive "buttery" quality. Stirred twice the next day. It was apparent in two days that MLF had started — carbonization was evident when the lees were stirred up.

9 WEEKS. Effervescence has been slowing of late. Now very little when I stir the lees.

10 WEEKS. No more effervescence. MLF complete-? TA = .73%, which is higher than I would expect after complete MLF. Moved to the garage to cold stabilize and start clarification. Wine tastes very dry, lacks fruit. Needs some character!

11 WEEKS. Chromatography test shows that MLF was just underway when it stopped. The temp. must have dropped lower than I realized (the carboys were sitting directly on the floor). Put the carboys back into the heated area, set on wood blocks to keep it off the floor. Raised ambient temp. to 80° and MLF re-started right away.

12 WEEKS. I stir the lees two or three times a week. The effervescence is a good sign of MLF.

14 WEEKS. Effervescence has slowed noticeably.

15 WEEKS. MLF complete. Set in a cool place to allow the gross lees to settle. Tastes thin, no fruit, does not seem to have much promise.

16 WEEKS. TA = .69%. Has some chardonnay character.

17 WEEKS. TA = .675% and .69%. pH = 3.39. RS is well under .05%. Tastes even better, like it has some potential! First racking — sulfited (1/4 tsp./7 gal.), added 8.75 g. of calcium carbonate to lower TA by about .05%, and fined with Sparkolloid (1 tsp./gal.). Brought inside so it will warm and clear faster.

19 WEEKS. Wine appears clear but still contains residual haze from Sparkolloid. Stuffed 2 cups of French oak splinters into one carboy, none in the other carboy.

6 MONTHS. Racked, adding 1.8 oz. of table sugar to the carboy with oak (to raise TA to about .2%), 1/8 tsp. sulfite and fined with 2 oz. of liquid beermaker's isinglass per carboy. The carboy without oak received 1.2 oz. of sugar for a different style.

8 MONTHS. Bottled with no further racking, even though there was visible haze. The necessary sulfite was added by rinsing the bottles with an intense sulfite solution, draining thoroughly and then adding 1 ml of premixed sulfite solution (1/4 tsp. sulfite per 25 ml water). The wine does not seem to have much fruit at this stage but probably will be very good in a couple of years.

FROZEN MUST

CABERNET SAUVIGNON
MALOLACTIC FERMENTATION
EXTENDED MACERATION

Day 1. Picked up 5 gal. frozen must, Sonoma Mountain Cabernet Sauvignon, with skins. Label: 26.5° B. sugar; .64 total acid; pH 3.45.

Day 2. Opened pail — mostly thawed. Added 1/4 tsp. sulfite.

Day 3. Completely thawed; almost to room temp. Stirred thoroughly. My readings: 22° B. sugar; approx. .9% total acid. (The variance from the label results because one bucket of grapes could have come from any corner of the vineyard and not reflect the average). The must has a great deal of flavor. Added 1 tsp. diammonium phosphate and pectic enzyme. Hydrated 1 pkg. Pasteur Red yeast in 1/2 cup warm water and sprinkled over surface.

DAY 4. Definitely starting to ferment — cap forming. Dumped from pail into 10 gal. primary fermenter and covered. Wine temp. is 67°. Took to small heated room which will be heated to approx. 75° for a few days, so the wine will ferment at 80 - 90°. Cap will be punched down twice daily from now on.

DAY 5. Fermenting vigorously. Wine temp. is 93°, so lowered the room temp. Added 1 tsp. yeast extract and malolactic starter.

DAY 8. Almost still. Wine temp. just under 80°. Wine should be tasted daily from now on to see when it mellows.

DAY 12. Very slight cap. RS over 1%, per Clinitest. Chromatography test shows ML is complete. Lowered room temp. to 70° B.

DAY 14. RS less than .5%. Seems to be still. Tastes more mellow —perhaps.

DAY 15. Tastes harsher - ? If this was the awaited mellowing, it was not very pronounced. Pressed out of concern about the mild hydrogen sulfide odor that has been present for the past several days. This was resulting from autolysis; i.e., active yeast cells consuming other yeast cells. (If the odor had been caused by excess sulfur on the grapes, there would have been an unmistakable rotten egg stink). To be on the safe side, I added .1 ppm of copper (.15 ml per gal. of 1% $CuSO_4 \cdot 5H_2O$). Ended up with 3 gal. + 750 ml + 375 ml. Set outside to cold stabilize and let gross lees settle.

4 WEEKS. First racking. There was so much pulp and lees that I got less than 2.8 gals. of wine from an original 5 gallons, which included skins. Very dark color.

7 WEEKS. Tests .72 TA; .2% RS; pH 3.55. It tastes acidic; the acid will probably need to be lowered.

11 WEEKS. TA tests .73%. TA must be lowered since it still tastes acidic. TA can be lowered chemically using potassium carbonate or with greater accuracy using calcium carbonate. Since the wine will not be bottled for several months, the calcium carbonate will have plenty of time to settle out. I would like to end up with TA just under .6%, but will err on the cautious side initially by adding only enough to lower it by .1%. (2.5 X 2.8 gal. = 7 g.). Dissolved the calcium carbonate in $\frac{1}{2}$ cup of water and added while racking. Set in the corner of a closet until the next racking — calcium carbonate will not precipitate at cold temperatures.

12 WEEKS. TA = .645%. Has nice bouquet, but not much flavor

13 WEEKS. TA = .67% pH = 3.80. Would like to lower the TA a bit more but will not tinker with it, since the pH is already higher than I would like. It does not taste acidic.

6 MONTHS. Racked.

9 MONTHS. Bottled. Due to the high pH, I used 75 ppm of sulfite at bottling.

RASPBERRY LIQUEUR

I make no fruit wines anymore, except this one. It is so good that I want to pass along my recipe for the "essence of raspberry," as I call it. If you like port wines or dessert wines, such as Sauternes, ice wines, late harvests, or sweet muscats, this should appeal to you.

If you reveal the recipe first, your friends are guaranteed to snicker. But not after they taste it! The secret is bananas. A pure raspberry liqueur without bananas would be one dimensional and unexceptional. The bananas broaden the raspberry flavor and round out the overall impression of the wine. The more bananas, the mellower the wine will be. Although the ratio of bananas to berries will have an effect on the flavor, the ratio is not critical to success. The following is only a suggestion to be followed on your first attempt. If you want a slightly different result the next time, change the recipe accordingly.

The goal is not to dilute the raspberry flavor and bouquet any more than necessary during the course of fermenting the alcohol level up to approximately 16%. Always try to minimize the amount of water added; try to get by with the liquid from the sugar syrup, the yeast starter and later from spiking it with Everclear or brandy. You don't get very much wine but the flavor is intense.

Here are the ingredients which will be needed initially:

1 flat fresh raspberries — approx. 12 lb.

5-7 lb. <u>ripe</u> bananas.

3 lb. raisins.

Pectic enzyme and potassium metabisulfite.

Sugar syrup.

Tokay yeast, which will ferment to a higher alcohol level than most other wine yeasts. Prise de Mousse would also be a good choice.

1 cup "Everclear" (190 proof ethanol) per gallon of finished wine or 2 cups of brandy.

Mash the raspberries in a small primary fermenter and add the raisins. Slice up the bananas and add them. Raspberries have wonderful flavor and bouquet but contain little sugar and little liquid. The raisins will be a source of sugar as they break down, but more sugar and a little more liquid will be needed. Make a very heavy sugar syrup by dissolving 4 pounds of cane or beet sugar in 2 quarts of boiling water. Add enough of it to the mashed fruit mixture to raise the Brix of the must to be approximately 35-40° B. The heat will help rehydrate the raisins and also help break down the berries. If the Brix is much above 40° after the mixture cools, add a little water to lower it. Store the extra syrup in the refrigerator for use later in fermenting or sweetening. After the mixture has cooled, add 1/8 tsp. of meta plus pectic enzyme.

Activate the yeast as described in Chapter 2 and inoculate the must when active. The cap should be punched down two or three times a day, as though red grapes were being fermented. This will extract more flavor out of the berries as well as frustrating the aerobic bacteria which might otherwise get established on top of the cap.

Check the remaining unfermented sugar with your saccharometer, and when it drops to 5° B., add more sugar syrup sufficient to raise it to 10 -15° B. Try not to exceed 15° B. because that seems to be the maximum desired sweetness in a fortified wine and very little of the additional sugar will ferment due to the high alcohol-sugar level.

When fermentation slows to the point where little CO_2 is being produced, pour the entire contents of the pail into a nylon mesh bag and press it by hand. (Using rubber gloves, of course). Then pour it into a small carboy or gallon jugs to finish fermenting. The jugs should be as full as possible. If you need to fill some air space, add more sliced bananas! Top with an air lock.

When fermentation has slowed to a trickle, it is time to fortify. You want to end up with a liqueur having an alcohol level of approximately 20%. At that level of alcohol, it will be stable and immune to air. This will require about 1 cup of Everclear or 2 cups of brandy per gallon. You also need to take the volume of pulp into account when spiking. If a fourth of the wine is pulp and solids, reduce the amount of alcohol to be added by one eighth. The solids will not absorb the alcohol, and you don't want the final product to be overly alcoholic.

You can leave it in the jugs to settle. The extensive volume of pulp will compact in a few weeks, and the liqueur will be clear and ready to bottle. This liqueur has a very intense bouquet, so I usually bottle in tenths rather than fifths, or even smaller bottles. The quantity is limited but the flavor is so intense that small bottles work well.

As mentioned, the final product can be altered by changing the ratio of the ingredients. My first effort consisted of equal amounts of berries, bananas and grapes. I added a small amount of water and sugar syrup as needed and spiked it. The resulting flavor was less concentrated than the above recipe, but I had more wine. It was indistinguishable from a high quality California port. Lower the ratio of bananas to berries and minimize the volume of water going in, and you get a more intense raspberry bouquet and flavor.

Blackberries could be used, but red raspberries are better. Black raspberries should also be good.

SOURCES and WEBSITES

FROZEN MUSTS

Peter Brehm has been crushing, pressing and freezing grape musts from Washington and California for many years. Local home winemakers arrange to pick up their fresh or frozen musts at his site; distant winemakers can have frozen musts shipped by UPS. He also sells through a few wine supply shops around the country that have freezer facilities and keep some in stock. It is an expensive proposition, but Brehm goes out of his way to deliver quality.

BREHM VINEYARDS
932 Evelyn Avenue
Albany, CA 94706
Phone: 510-527-3675
FAX: 510-526-1372
E-mail: PbrehmVin@aol.com

ASEPTIC JUICES AND CONCENTRATE KITS

There may be other companies marketing concentrate kits, but this is a list of the larger ones. Although they are Canadian companies, they all have U.S. wholesalers who sell to local beer and wine supply stores and would be happy to send literature and put you in touch with their U.S. outlets. Your local wine supply shop will also know how to order for you.

BREW KING
1622 Kebet Way
Port Coquitlam, BC
CANADA V3C 5W9
Phone: (604) 464-1882
FAX: (604) 941-9811
E-mail: brew-king@brewking.com/

MOSTI MONDIALE INC.
6865 Route 132
Ville Ste. Catherine, QC
CANADA J0L 1E0
Phone: (514) 638-6380
FAX: (541) 638-7049
E-mail: webmaster@mostimondiale.com
Website: www.mostimondiale.com/

R J GRAPE PRODUCTS
1570 King E
Kitchener, ON
CANADA N2G 2P1
Phone: (519) 743-3755
FAX: 1-888-602-7777
E-mail: info@rjgrape.com
Website: www.rjgrape.com/

VINECO INTERNATIONAL PRODUCTS
27 Scott W.
St. Catharines, ON
CANADA L2R 6W8
Phone: (905) 685-9342
FAX: (905) 685-9551
E-mail: hindm@cadvision.com
Website: www.vineco.on.ca

VINOTHEQUE WINE MAKING SUPPLIES
2142 South Service Road Trans-Canada Hwy
Dorval, QC
CANADA H9P 2N4
Phone: (514) 684-1331
FAX: 1-800-363-1506
E-mail: vinotheque@interlink.net/
Website: www.vinotheque.net/

WINE ART
55 Clegg Road
Markham, ON
CANADA L6G 1B9
Phone: 1-888-477-9463
FAX: 905-477-9232
E-mail: wineart@veccon.on.ca
Website: www.wineart.com/

WEBSITES OF INTEREST

http://www.vicon.net/~aws/	American WineSociety
http://www.wineserver.ucdavis.edu/	University of California at Davis
http://www.lallemand.com/	Lalvin Yeasts
http://www.scottlab.com/	Scott Laboratories
http://www.wyeastlab.com/	Wyeast Labs
http://www.makewine.com	Amateur Winemakers of Ontario
http://www.bcwine.vawa	Vancouver Amatuer Winemakers Assn
http://www.lafn/community/cellarmasters	Cellarmasters
http://www.tomatoweb.com/shw	Sacramento Home Winemakers

TABLE OF EQUIVALENTS

1 oz.=28.4g.   1 g. = .0353 oz.
1 lb.=454g.   1 kg. =2.20lb.
1 fl. oz. =29.6 ml   1 gal. = 128 oz.=3.785L.
1 qt.=.95L.

One part per million is either 1 gram per million milliliters or 1 milliliter per million milliliters. If you seek a particular level of an active chemical, such as potassium metabisulfite, you have to adjust. In the case of meta, for example, only half the weight becomes free SO2. So you have to add twice as much to reach the desired level.

1 part per million = .001 g/L. = .019 g/5 gal.
1 part per million = 1 ml/264 gal.

TO RAISE TOTAL ACID BY .1%

tartaric acid -- add 3.8 g/gal.
malic acid -- add 3.4 g/gal.

TO LOWER TOTAL ACID BY .1%

calcium carbonate -- add 2.5 g./gal.
potassium carbonate -- add 3.8 g./gal.
potassium bicarbonate -- add 3.4 g./ gal.

TO CONVERT BRIX TO SPECIFIC GRAVITY

$$\text{Brix} = \frac{261.3}{\text{sp.grav.}} \quad (@\ 68°\ F.)$$

Index